IN
REMEMBRANCE
OF HIM

Classics of Reformed Spirituality

This series offers fresh translations of key writings from the seventeenth and eighteenth centuries, making them accessible to the twenty-first century church. These writings from the "Further Reformation" in the Netherlands offer a balance of doctrine and piety, a mingling of theology and life that has seldom been equaled in the history of Christianity. Each book in this series will provide invaluable insight into a vibrant part of the Christian heritage.

Other Books in the Series:

IN
REMEMBRANCE
OF HIM

PROFITING FROM THE LORD'S SUPPER

Guilelmus Saldenus
& Wilhelmus à Brakel

Translated by Bartel Elshout
Edited by James A. DeJong

REFORMATION HERITAGE BOOKS
Grand Rapids, Michigan

In Remembrance of Him
© 2012 by the Dutch Reformed Translation Society

Published by
REFORMATION HERITAGE BOOKS
2965 Leonard St. NE
Grand Rapids, MI 49525
616-977-0889 / Fax 616-285-3246
e-mail: orders@heritagebooks.org
website: www.heritagebooks.org

Printed in the United States of America
12 13 14 15 16 17/10 9 8 7 6 5 4 3 2 1

Library of Congress Cataloging-in-Publication Data

In remembrance of Him : profiting from the Lord's Supper / Guilelmus Saldenus & Wilhelmus à Brakel ; translated by Bartel Elshout ; edited by James A. De Jong.
    p. cm. — (Classics of Reformed spirituality)
    Includes bibliographical references (p.   ).
    ISBN 978-1-60178-173-4 (pbk. : alk. paper) 1. Lord's Supper—Reformed Church—Early works to 1800. I. Elshout, Bartel, 1949- II. De Jong, James A., 1941- III. Saldenus, Guilielmus, 1627-1694. Kracht des Avondmaals. English. IV. Brakel, Wilhelmus à, 1635-1711. Stichtelijke oefeningen. English.
    BV825.3.I513 2012
    234'.163—dc23
                              2012008233

Contents

Edifying Discourses Regarding the Preparation for, the Partaking of, and the Reflection upon the Sacrament of the Lord's Supper

by Wilhelmus à Brakel

Introduction

The Lord's Supper and Essays for Self-Examination

The two seventeenth-century essays translated and offered in this book were originally designed to help people of the Dutch Further Reformation derive the greatest benefit from celebrating the Lord's Supper. They aimed at preparing these devout Reformed Christians for the sacrament. They were intended to foster understanding of what to expect or not expect in the supper itself. And they instructed them in how to follow up the meal in a spiritually beneficial manner. As such, these two contributions are but two examples of a much larger genre of edifying Lord's Supper literature that developed in the Netherlands in the seventeenth century.

Why was this significant, sustained attention to the sacrament produced? One only needs to recall that throughout the Middle Ages an awesome fear of the sacrament developed. By the late centuries of that era, the doctrine of transubstantiation was entrenched in Vatican thought. The great mystery of the physical elements being miraculously changed into the real body and blood of Christ was accentuated ritually and approached with liturgical solemnity. The clergy prepared carefully for officiating at this event. People had to make honest, full confession beforehand and had to complete prescribed penance lest they suffer eternal consequences. Neglect of this sure means of conveying saving grace as well as cavalier participation in the sacrament were equally risky. No wonder the altar rail was approached with trepidation. Barring the laity from celebrating with both elements only underscored the danger of profaning this culmination of Christian worship.

The sixteenth-century Reformers devoted vast attention biblically to correcting the theology of the Lord's Supper and to re-educating believers in its meaning and observance. No wonder a disproportionate amount of attention is paid the supper in Reformation confessions, commentaries, doctrinal works, conversations and colloquies, polemics, and liturgical practice. The Lord's Supper was at the core of the differences between Rome and the Reformation. But correcting a misguided understanding and practice of this sacrament did not lessen the gravity of the event; it only accentuated it. Christians needed to come to absolute clarity on what coming to the table meant. They had to be disabused of the spiritually destructive errors ingrained in them. But they also had to approach so important an event in a thoroughly chastened spirit. Doing any less meant "eating and drinking judgment unto themselves," in the words of Paul, which became the governing passage for fencing the table. The essays presented in this volume reflect that emphasis. It is an emphasis that defined Protestant, including Dutch Reformed and Puritan, sacramental thought and practice into the recent modern era.

The Guilelmus Saldenus essay concentrates on two themes: joy or comfort in celebrating the sacrament and the holiness or sanctified living that it ought to generate. The theme of joy is remarkable, since it shatters the image or caricature of Further Reformation folk as dour legalists. But the joy is not a superficial or frivolous emotion; it is a deep, inner elation and assurance of well-being based on the finished work of the cross. Solemnity is no enemy of such overwhelming comfort; it is rather the respectful atmosphere in which it should be experienced and appreciated. What is quite remarkable in Saldenus's explanation is that comfort and joy should not be misunderstood as the subjective moods or dispositions with which one approaches or leaves the table. These may vary due to immediate circumstances, but the deeper sense of well-being signified and sealed in the Lord's Supper will endure and must be the celebrant's focus. In fact, the author repeatedly warns against staying away from the table based on fluctuating human emotions. One ought to come seeking fortified faith that rests on divine promises. Passages in Chapter 5 that deal with the believer's participation in the sufferings of Christ via a properly prepared celebration of the sacrament are some of the most vivid and moving expositions of communing with the Lord one can find in devotional literature anywhere. Saldenus obviously reflected deeply and perceptively on the subject.

The Wilhelmus à Brakel essay consists of three discourses in catechetical form, which was typical of instructional or edifying literature of the era. As the title indicates, they deal with preparation for the celebration, the celebration itself, and the post-communion response to having been at the table. This three-step pattern was also captured in the typical Dutch Reformed practice of preaching a preparatory sermon the week before communion Sunday, preaching a communion sermon at the communion service, and preaching a post-communion or applicatory sermon at the evening service on communion Sunday. À Brakel's discourses may well have been intended to be read and reflected upon in conjunction with these services. This material was presented for publication, along with a 1702 meditation, by his grandson in 1751, years after à Brakel had died.

While the Lord's Supper is commonly celebrated with much more frequency today than four times a year, which was the prevailing practice in the Dutch Reformed tradition well into the modern era, it is also usually observed without the kind of deep reflection presented in these essays. By making them available for the first time in English, we hope and pray that they will contribute to a richer celebration of the sacrament for the reader.

Guilelmus Antonius Saldenus

Guilelmus Saldenus lived from 1627 to 1694. After his theological training in Utrecht, he was a lifelong pastor: Renswoude (1649), Kockengen (1652), Enkhuizen (1655), Delft (1664), and The Hague (1677). At Utrecht, he studied under Gisbertus Voetius and Johannes Hoornbeeck, two other authors featured in the series of titles on spiritual formation in which the present volume appears. While he never became a theological professor, he did stay theologically engaged during his pastorates. The various titles he produced are marked by insight and balance, as is the material on the Lord's Supper presented here. The faculty at Utrecht respected him so highly that it accorded him an honorary doctorate, a tribute only very rarely granted in the seventeenth century. His material is largely edifying and devotional in nature. It was reprinted and read with appreciation by many into the

Guiljelmus Saldenus (1627–1694)

nineteenth century, when it contributed to the revival of confessional
Reformed spirituality.

The tone of Saldenus's piety was individualistic and oriented
toward the hereafter, according to Wilhelm Goeters, who has
given this author's works particularly close scrutiny. A frequently
reprinted and read Saldenus title dealt with the road or way of life.
It was subtitled "a short [650 pages!], simple introduction to the
nature and characteristics of the true power of salvation." Another
title dealt with "spiritual honey" in a collection of sermons. Another
was called a "touchstone for Christian discernment" and dealt with
spiritual self-assessment and the ability to discern the spirituality
of others. "The way of comfort revealed for penitent believers" was
yet another title in the Saldenus oeuvre. "The saints' lamentations
on the bitterness of Zion's misery" dealt with the sorry state of the
church in the Netherlands. Nor did Saldenus ignore children; he
produced material for their instruction in the Christian faith. He
was an effective preacher who emphasized the need for conversion,
a holy walk with the Lord, and great anticipation of the blessedness

awaiting God's children in the life to come. As already noted in connection with his work on the Lord's Supper, he stressed that the believer's conviction and assurance do not rest on religious feelings or subjective dispositions, however powerful these may sometimes be, but on the objective promises and saving work of God in Christ. Saldenus was appreciated for his spiritual and theological balance as well as for flashes of unusual spiritual perceptivity.

Wilhelmus à Brakel

Only slightly younger than Saldenus, Wilhelmus à Brakel lived from 1635 until 1711. The son of a prominent minister in the Further Reformation tradition, he was trained for ministry at Franeker and Utrecht, where he was deeply influenced by Voetius. He served congregations in Exmorra (1662), Stavoren (1665), Harlingen (1670), Leeuwarden (1673), and Rotterdam (1683). He was a gifted and much appreciated preacher. Initially inclined toward the mystical features of Labadism, he in time came to understand and to warn in print against the separatism of that movement. He advocated conventicles as effective instruments for cultivating deeper, more reflective spirituality, inspiration, instruction in the faith, supportive fellowship, and fervent prayer life. These were private, weekday services that were controversial because consistories and civil authorities often perceived them to be an indictment on the official public worship and church life of the Dutch Reformed Church. "Father à Brakel's" public opposition to the role of Dutch civil officials in both approving ministers called to serve in congregations and at times dismissing them from service made him controversial. The role of civil authorities in Dutch church life had been a long-standing thorn in the side of Reformed leaders, however, but à Brakel's popularity and measured restraint protected him from removal.

Like that of Voetius, his mentor, his preaching and writing were an appealing blend of confessional Reformed orthodoxy and explicitly concrete spiritual practice. In fact, his followers, an unusually extensive group, were known as Brakelian Voetians. His publications were widely read and frequently reprinted deep into the nineteenth century.

À Brakel's most important and extensive work is his *Reasonable Christianity* (*Redelijke Godsdienst*). The first two of its three parts were first translated into English as *The Christian's Reasonable Service* (4 vols.) in the last two decades of the twentieth century. Two-thirds of part three consists of a commentary on the book of Revelation. The subtitle of this material identifies it as "a work in which the divine truths of

Wilhelmus à Brakel (1635–1711)

the covenant of grace are explained." The first edition of *Reasonable Christianity* appeared in 1700, near the end of his long career. By the next year it had to be reprinted. Then it was expanded for its third appearance shortly thereafter. It enjoyed some twenty reprints in the eighteenth century alone. It was one of the most frequently cited works of "the old authors," as Further Reformation writers were called by Dutch-speaking American religious writers in the nineteenth century. Far from being academic theology, the work might well be called "applied devotional theology" for its blend of doctrine and Christian living. Part one is a readable, popular-level explanation and application of forty-two main doctrinal topics (loci) of the Christian faith; it comes to just over a thousand pages. Part two is entirely on living the sanctified life as understood by explaining the Ten Commandments, the main spiritual affections, the Lord's Prayer, classic Christian virtues, spiritual struggles, perseverance, and the doctrine of the last things; it comes to almost seven hundred pages. Part three is a survey of redemptive history from creation through the

New Testament church and culminates with the lengthy commentary on the book of Revelation; it comes to three hundred and fifty pages, two hundred of them devoted to the commentary. It was probably the most widely read and consulted work of its kind in Dutch Reformed circles through the nineteenth century.

Another popular title by the same author is *The True Christian or Upright Believer,* a collection of ten sermons. *Hallelujah! Or, Praising the Lord* deals with the administration of the covenant of grace in both the Old and New Testaments. *The Lord Jesus Christ, the Only and Sovereign Lord of the Church* appeared in 1688. His first wife, Sarah Nevius, was a popular Christian writer in her own right. Her book *An Attentive Student of the Lord Jesus* enjoyed wide circulation and was frequently reprinted. All of these titles represent the devotional and edifying literature of the Dutch Further Reformation and solidified à Brakel's reputation as one of the pre-eminent leaders of that movement.

Technical Points

A few technical points deserve brief comment. The two essays are replete with biblical quotations. These do not always clearly connect with the point the author is making. Rather than delete them, we have left them in the text since, often with a little more reflection, the modern reader can discover what was on the writer's mind. We have changed verse numbers to accord with English-language numbering where it varies from Dutch numbering. Where the authors give an erroneous reference or omit a reference, we have corrected the error or included the reference in a footnote. Both the translator and the editor have carefully reviewed the biblical references. The English translations of Scripture are our own.

We have not included laudatory poems or ecclesiastical endorsements, both of which typically appeared in seventeenth- and eighteenth-century religious literature of the type presented here. We have left in the text occasional Latin phrases or terms. In the case of the Saldenus material, we have worked from a late-seventeenth-century printing. In the case of the à Brakel material, we have relied on a 1985 Dutch reprint by the publisher Den Hertog in Houten, the Netherlands, and edited by Rev. C. J. Meeuwse. Finally, where the author has mixed the singular and the plural grammatically, we have left his choices uncorrected; this captures his attempt to personalize the material for the reader. As editor, I commend Rev. Bartel Elshout for capturing the tone and spirit of the material. His

thorough familiarity with the Dutch devotional literature of the
period is obvious in his excellent work. The reader is referred to his
website noted in the bibliography. Here he presents a longer review of
à Brakel's life than I have provided in this introduction. The site also
includes our colleague Dr. Joel's Beeke's balanced, comprehensive
essay on the Further Reformation. Both of these pieces are from
the English translation of à Brakel's work noted below. The site also
contains a brief video clip of Elshout commending the work.

James A. De Jong

EFFICACY OF THE LORD'S SUPPER

TO THE COMFORT AND SANCTIFICATION OF GOD'S CHILDREN

Briefly Addressed by

Guilelmus Saldenus

Minister of the Gospel in Delft

Published according to
Article 55 of the Church Order

Dedication to Mr. Frederick Budens
Formerly a Magistrate of Bergen op Zoom

Your Honor,

This present treatise, as you can observe, deals with the Lord's Supper and how the godly must thereby be comforted and sanctified. It is certainly a subject that has been addressed by so many in a variety of ways—and rightfully so. Each author, in his own way, has done his best to present this delightful meal in the most glorious and delectable terms. In this I have always been able to detect a special token of God's love, however much one may deem this to be *actum agere*, that is, repetitive. The desires and inclinations of man vary, and everyone does not enjoy the same dish in identical fashion. What matters is whether the food is good; that is, holy and yielding spiritual blessing. What else is it but a proof of God's lovingkindness that everyone can find his delight in this meal?

Besides, it rarely happens that everyone writes the identical thing about a common subject. The concepts addressed generally vary considerably. Due to the sovereign ministry of the Holy Spirit, the one sees and finds something in God's Word that others have not perceived in the same fashion.

Therefore, following many who are preeminent among the people, I have also composed something regarding this heavenly subject, having no other objective than by way of a few propositions and instructions to set before the common people as clearly as possible the nature and proper observance of the Lord's Supper. I readily admit that I am not presenting something new. I would, however, rather walk upon the established, and thus the safest, path. *Via trita via tuta.* Though the method I use regarding this subject matter is perhaps not the most original, and on occasion could easily suggest another approach or insight that has not been brought forward by others, it may yet not be entirely unsuitable, particularly for concerned Christians.

Section one has already been published over a period of four years under the title *A Spiritual Supper*, however, without any reference to the author's name. To this I now add section two, so that a Christian in these few pages may be furnished with all that is important and essential to achieve the most important objectives of the Lord's Supper: comfort and sanctification.

In this treatise, my focus is primarily on comfort and secondarily on sanctification, not because comfort should be preferred before sanctification, but rather because I already had begun to follow this order. It also occurs to me that comfort is as much a fruit of the Lord's Supper as is sanctification, though these two influence each other. I am generally short and simple in my approach, leaving all extensive and soul-stirring exposition to others. I do this in recognition of the fact one can hardly find a better and more notable exposition than the writings of W. Teellinck, Hildersham, Derlincourt, Moulin, Jeremiah Dijke, D. Simonides, etc. It is also not so much my objective to move people as it is to instruct, and thus to provide small portions of that which could be enlarged upon considerably.

As a remedy for all the doubts of a child of God regarding either his state in general or that which is the result of inner strife, I do not wish to recommend anything other than the excellent, concise, and very scriptural treatise of my highly esteemed and honorable fellow laborer, Rev. Hermannus Tegularius, entitled *Scriptural Marks of a True Christian*. I especially recommend the second edition, which has been expanded considerably, and do not doubt but that everyone will be able to find instruction in this that suits him personally.

My sole objective is to resolve concerns in regard to the Lord's Supper—those matters that would inhibit the comfort and sanctification of God's children.

Having said this, your honor, I want to address you in particular. For a number of reasons, I consider it to be my obligation to dedicate these humble meditations respectfully to your honor. First, I am deeply obliged to you for the numerous and gracious favors and courtesies my family and I have so frequently enjoyed in your home. I have never had a suitable opportunity to express my gratitude for this.

Another reason is that I know your honor to be a lover of God's church and the doctrine of salvation. Considering your godly disposition, I am therefore hopeful that your honor will not only be pleased with this little treatise, but that it may also in some small measure be profitable to your soul.

Finally, I pray that the God of all grace will strengthen your honor in that regard by His Spirit, and that, after having often partaken of this external supper with a sanctified heart, you may once be seated in the heavens at His eternal supper with Abraham, Isaac, and Jacob.

I hereby conclude, and as a friend and servant of your honor, I remain,

G. Saldenus
Delft, August 25, 1664

Part I:
On Comfort

———————— ✳ ————————

CHAPTER

1

❋

All religious duties have two objectives, the primary being God's honor and the secondary being the spiritual profit of man. Therefore, in all that he does, a Christian must have these two objectives in view, though there must be a distinction between them. Without having these two in view, he will be incapable of doing any good. He must either deny his obligatory love toward God or his love for himself, and it is entirely fitting and essential that the first objective have the preeminence. Thus, when contrasted, this second objective should yield and be subordinate to the first. Yes, if one of the two would have to be the lesser, that is, if the choice would be between God's honor and man's spiritual well-being, man should rather yield and minimize that which is his rather than having God not receive His worthy due. This does not mean, however, that he should either ignore or neglect his own interest. Rather, in all humility he should do his utmost not only to strive for God's honor in all that he does, but also seek to attain the greatest joy and benefit for himself. He may do so not only when prayerfully reading, hearing, and meditating upon God's Word, but especially when partaking of the Holy Supper of the Lord.

This Christian duty, more so than is true for all other duties, has been ordained and instituted by God for man's spiritual joy and strengthening. Therefore, we believe it to be most appropriate to posit that though the honor of God must always have the preeminence, we must also seek to secure that which is to our benefit and to lay out before you the sure and spiritual way in which we may obtain it. We are prompted to do this since many are accustomed to lament the lack of fruit in connection with the Lord's Supper.

I will not address here the comfort of the soul and its sanctification in general, but only the Lord's Supper's efficacy in stimulating and increasing such comfort and sanctification of man as issue forth from and flourish as a fruit of the Lord's Supper.

Regarding both matters, we will proceed as follows:

I.   We will present several general propositions regarding these spiritual fruits, and then expose each error made in that regard.

II.   We will prescribe directions and means, so that such spiritual fruits may be derived from the Lord's Supper.

III. We will respond to several objections regarding this.

Proposition #1: It is a special fruit and consequence of the lawful partaking of the Lord's Supper that it generates comfort and joy in the hearts of God's children (Rom. 4:11; 1 Cor. 10:16–17; 1 Cor. 5:7; Song 5:1; etc.).

This brings to the fore:

1. the misunderstanding of those who partake of the Lord's Supper for no other reason than that they see others do likewise; or because they wish to pursue some temporary advantage, honor, and/or position; or because they wish to quiet their consciences, who perhaps are convinced that they no longer can be at peace in neglecting the same; or because of some other carnal motives, without there being anything memorable or delightful in it for them. Such people are generally satisfied if they have merely engaged in the outward act, even though they have never desired or perceived the least stirring of the soul. We will demonstrate, however, that this ought to be the special fruit of the Lord's Supper. How wretched are those who are of such a disposition! Concerning such we fear that since they do not seek any spiritual joy in and by means of the Lord's Supper (and if they do not change in that regard), this will be a certain indication of their

ultimate end and eternal sorrow. Paul says concerning them that they eat and drink judgment to themselves, not discerning the Lord's body (1 Cor. 11:29).

2. that there are those who, though they are godly, fail to partake of the Lord's Supper with the objective of stirring up in themselves, as they ought to, this spiritual joy; and if they persist in this, they will always remain mired (I know not due to what sort of grievous misunderstanding) in a despondent questioning, languishing, muddling, etc. I am not speaking of those who do their utmost in wrestling to overcome this, but rather, who, sad to say, frequently give in to such negative thought patterns. This is lamented in these words, "And there is none that…stirs up himself to take hold of you" (Isa. 64:7)—as if God would be well served by petulant and disagreeable guests who are always sighing! We would rather not admonish such troubled and despondent souls. However, since they frequently give in too much to this despondency, we can therefore not refrain from addressing these errors, for thereby they greatly and grievously shortchange the kindness of God and the grace within them, causing their own heart as well as their spiritual vitality to dwindle and languish (Ps. 77:10).

Proposition #2: This comforting joy of the Lord's Supper must not be considered as something external or physical, but rather, as something internal and spiritual (Ps. 4:8; Luke 1:47; Ps. 22:27).

This joy essentially consists of these three components:

1. It consists of a clearer and more distinct apprehension of the magnitude and preciousness of the suffering of Jesus Christ. This is set before us in the Lord's Supper not merely as is done and taught through the Word, nor is this embraced as being true by faith only. Rather, it is set before us as something that is seen, tasted, and felt through the administration of tangible and visible signs, and thus by taking, breaking, giving, pouring, eating, and drinking, etc., of the bread and wine.

2. It consists in a greater and more certain peace of heart proceeding from and by way of an assured fellowship with the all-sufficient

merits of Jesus Christ. In the Lord's Supper, by way of various ceremonial actions, all of this is displayed much more visibly and clearly, and it is bound upon the soul in a very personal way.

3. It consists of a fuller peace and inner satisfaction and of a determination to obey in return this perfectly obedient Christ, and if necessary to die, be broken, etc., for Him who died such a death, was broken, and whom one has eaten by faith (2 Cor. 5:15).[1]

All of these matters are to be found in a spiritual Christian prior to his partaking of the Lord's Supper. However, in the Lord's Supper he experiences this in a more lively and experiential manner. It is the latter that constitutes his spiritual joy.

This, in turn, exposes the lamentable error:

1. of those who always imagine something carnal and physical, and who even appear to be of the opinion that a good Lord's Supper consists of a good meal and that this would be the true joy with which one would respond to this holy activity. Or, if they are not that foolish, they will at least enjoy a carnal security (assuming that the record of their sins is thereby abolished) and sit quietly at the Lord's Table without any serious concern for the means of grace. Truly, such are carnal and natural men who do not have the Spirit (Jude 19). And since they neither have spiritual eyes nor spiritual hearts, they would like to conform everything, and especially this spiritual meal, to their own state; they would thus turn it into an entirely carnal event. How poor is such a soul who subjects this heavenly work to shame and ignominy, and leads herself to perdition!

A true partaker of the Lord's Supper does not seek external joy. He neither feels nor displays it, except insomuch as perhaps it would be to the edification and inspiration of others. "The kingdom of God is not meat and drink; but righteousness, and peace, and joy in the Holy Spirit" (Rom. 14:17).

---

1. Sometimes seventeenth-century biblical references seem oblique, as here. Saldenus sees a parallel here and in this verse between Christ's death and His followers' willingness to die to self. While many following biblical citations may be even more baffling to today's reader, a little deeper reflection will often disclose what the author probably had in mind.

2. of those who are not looking for something external but nevertheless remain greatly ensnared by their feelings, believing that there is no other source of joy in the Lord's Supper except that they feel and are aware of a sensible impression of such and such a matter. Or, to say it even more clearly, such a soul wants her affections to be touched, moved, stroked, and stimulated in a measure as she has seen at times and detected in herself or in others. It is true that the joy of which we are speaking can be so abundant that it often stirs up the affections. However, this should not be viewed as normative. Much less should it be concluded that where this is lacking there would also be no spiritual joy in the heart. The seat of this joy is not in the affections, etc., but rather, in the rational faculties of the soul, that is, in the intellect and the will. Such partakers will be filled with the greatest measure of joy even in the complete absence of all that is sensual. Peter speaks of this: "Though now you do not see him, yet believing, you rejoice with joy unspeakable and full of glory" (1 Peter 1:8).

Proposition #3: None other than the truly converted can be partakers of this spiritual comfort and joy in the Lord's Supper (1 Cor. 11:28; 2 Chron. 31:18; 2 Cor. 6:14–15; 1 Cor. 10:19–20; Ps. 15:1–2; etc.).

This confirms the following:

1. What a grievous thing it is at times that many people are so rashly invited and admitted to the Lord's Table, and then so readily attend! Often there is not the least evidence of true contrition and faith. Except for some lofty words, they often do not conduct themselves any differently than purely carnal and worldly people. That which is holy ought not to be given unto the dogs, neither should these pearls be cast before swine (1 Cor. 11:28).

The Lord's Supper is not a means to bestow grace upon someone, but rather to strengthen existing grace, which is assumed to be present in those who lawfully partake of the Lord's Supper. To partake is indeed a duty incumbent upon all of Christianity, and believers are even commanded to do so. However, one can partake neither lawfully nor profitably unless conversion has truly occurred. It is therefore all the more surprising that, generally speaking, such carnal and smooth-speaking individuals are even more boastful than others about their spiritual joy and ecstasy, although there is no portion in it for them but only for the truly converted. "Light is sown for the righteous, and gladness for the upright in heart" (Ps. 97:11).

2. However much the true sheep may go astray, such as are truly contrite and broken because of their sins and who by a true faith, however weak that faith may be, are grafted into Christ often dare not number themselves among those who know of such joy; this is due to the perception of their unworthiness and deficiencies. They are of the opinion that this is not for them, but rather only for those who in all things conduct themselves better than they do. How sad this is, as it proceeds from a serious misunderstanding. The fact is that this joy is the lawful portion of all who have humbled themselves and have repented; yes, as we have just stated, it is for none other but those (2 Cor. 7:6).[2] As imperfect as their conversion may be, it cannot take away the fact that such are partakers of such joy. This is their portion, not because of the perfection of their conversion, but rather for the sake of Christ's merits. We may and must conclude from their conversion that all these benefits are theirs. "If you believe with all your heart, you may" (Acts 8:37). If they would not view themselves as unworthy, they would neither be able to desire nor obtain this joy in the right way. In so doing, they would remain focused on themselves and not seek Christ, who nevertheless is the eternal fountain of this joy (Ps. 36:10).

Proposition #4: This spiritual joy derived from the Lord's Supper will ordinarily only be experienced by those who have actively prepared themselves for it (2 Chron. 30:18–20; 1 Cor. 11:28; 2 Cor. 9:6; 2 Chron. 30:3).

---

2. See note 1 above. Paul is "lawfully" joyful because of Titus's coming to him, just as the dubious but lawful celebrant of the Lord's Supper ought to feel joyful at the table.

1. When saying that this joy "will ordinarily only be experienced by those, etc." we imply that God can at times grant this in an extraordinary manner. Though we cannot limit Him in that regard, we are not to consider this as normative.

2. We also maintain that those who experience this joy must indeed be prepared (1 Cor. 11:28). Such habitual preparation is in essence no different from conversion itself, of which we have spoken earlier. To be prepared in very deed means that a believer, according to the measure of grace derived from Christ, has stirred up all these good virtues and dispositions such as knowledge, desire, faith, love, obedience, etc., that have been planted in him in conversion. He does so with immediate application and appropriation in regard to the special activity of the Lord's Supper.

In regard to this, they deceive themselves

1. who partake of the Lord's Supper unmoved and unfit, and thus without any premeditation as to what they are doing and how they are to conduct themselves. How grievously do such take hold of and trample upon that which is holy, doing so with unclean and unwashed hands and feet. Ought not many to be counted among such wretched souls, who, rather than receiving the Lord Jesus by way of the bread and wine, due to their willful lack of preparation, permit Satan with all his vile operations to penetrate the soul? Such may eat indeed, but they cannot be satisfied (Hos. 4:10). And though they speak of joy, as they often do, it is nothing more than a satanic lullaby. Theirs is the portion of one whose hunger is counterfeit, who is dreaming that he is eating and being satisfied. Once he awakens, he will find his soul to be empty after all (Isa. 29:8; John 13:27).

2. who are not as brazen as those whom we have just described, but who nevertheless engage in their preparation in a careless and carnal manner. They prepare themselves in a manner to which they are accustomed in the performance of all their religious duties, but their preparation lacks the dignity and solemnity that this special meal demands. Therefore, they ordinarily leave the table so void of fruit and joy.

God generally gives a measure of spiritual joy that is proportionate to the measure of our preparation, and if the latter is lacking, the first will ordinarily be withheld as well. He will spread His hands of blessing over us if we have examined our hearts extensively before Him regarding His work. However, that which is true for all other religious duties is applicable here as well: He at times will give nothing to one who has prepared himself most thoroughly so that one's preparation will not be viewed as the meriting cause of His lovingkindness. However, if He gives nothing to the one who has neglected to prepare himself, then he must generally consider his lack of preparation as the cause of such spiritual leanness (Ps. 81:11).

Proposition #5: This spiritual joy, derived from the Lord's Supper, will ordinarily not be experienced as generously by the person who finds himself in a troubled and confused state as by those whose condition is stable and tranquil (Eph. 1:10; Ps. 40:13).

It is therefore a fault

1. of some that exert themselves so little to foster and preserve a good spiritual disposition. How few pay attention to this matter! Are we not commonly very much engaged in having everything in our homes, yards, and bedrooms arranged in an orderly fashion, but not in regard to our soul? And thus, that which is most precious (our soul) we permit to be most neglected and unkept. This is frequently the cause why one does not derive as much joy or comfort from the Lord's Supper as he ought. It is true for all meals that when confusion and disorder prevail, joy and satisfaction will decrease proportionately. Such as pay little attention to this will rob themselves of a great advantage. They, so to speak, chase God completely from their souls. This is contrary to what is generally true, namely, something that the apostle at a special occasion says regarding Him: "God is not the author of confusion, but of peace" (1 Cor. 14:33).

2. of others whose souls for a long time have been assaulted and troubled, and who are wondering so much why they have attended the Lord's Supper so frequently, and yet always without any

enjoyment and delight. Often the cause is to be found in their disconcerted and troubled condition. As stated earlier, this spiritual joy consists primarily in a clear perception of the mystery of Christ's suffering and our personal interest in it. However, the spiritual eyes of those who are so greatly troubled are as it were closed, and therefore they lack the ability to grasp matters as they ought. Should it then be a surprise that they do not experience this joy? David says, "My iniquities have taken hold of me, so that I am not able to look up" (Ps. 40:12). It is not good that such are overly concerned about this. No, no! Let them take courage! And as soon as their condition has become more stable, this darkness will lift and their light will break forth as the sun. And indeed, the LORD did ultimately answer Job out of the whirlwind (Job 38:1).

Proposition #6: All Christians will not derive the same measure of this spiritual joy from the Lord's Supper (1 Cor. 12:6; 1 Cor. 15:31; 2 Cor. 12:23).

From this it follows that they are very much in error who

1. frequently, due to a lesser measure of this spiritual joy, question the genuineness of such joy. "For," so they say, "the measure of my joy is not as others experience it, and therefore what I have must be discounted." To draw such a conclusion is like saying, "I do not have as much money as either Croesus or Solomon, and thus my money is worthless." Who in their right mind would draw such a conclusion? Such reasoning is like putting the cart before the horse. The Lord does not consider something good because of its measure, but because He values the smallest good thing as great when it is done in uprightness. Who would then despise the day of small things (Zech. 4:10)? God in His wisdom gives more to one than to another, in each case in a measure suitable to the person, and therefore we must leave that matter in His hands (1 Cor. 12:7).

2. make their satisfaction generally too dependent on a specific measure of this spiritual comfort. This often results in grumbling and complaining when their measure of joy is not what they desire it to be. Experience teaches that even healthy believers do not

learn all that much in this regard. However, in so doing they also are guilty of challenging God's absolute wisdom and of attempting in various ways to compel Him to conform to their wishes. God is a wise dispenser of His gifts, and He may therefore, as He once said, "do what I will with my own" (Matt. 20:15). When one seeks to limit Him, He will generally withdraw His hand from such people as would establish their own standards. If, however, He is yet pleased to grant some measure of joy, then their displeasure regarding the measure of joy they have received will result in the substance of it being either quenched or extinguished.

Proposition #7: This joy proceeding from the Lord's Supper is not limited to the time when one either partakes or has partaken of this Supper. Rather, it can also be first felt or noticed long thereafter (John 10:41; 2 Sam. 10:1, 6, 9).

It can therefore be observed that it is a serious error

1. when many so readily conclude that there is no comfort for them in the Lord's Supper because, either when or after partaking, they were not aware or did not become aware of such joy. As if God the Lord is limited to any precise moment! It is true, however, that He most commonly works this contemporaneously with the use of the means in order thereby to recommend and validate their use all the more. Yet, He has not bound Himself to them in such an absolute sense as if He never could or would follow a different course (Matt. 16:10; Acts 16:14). Frequently, during the Lord's Supper—or when we are engaged in prayer, or during our reading and hearing of His Word, or when we are engaged in some other profitable exercises—He may act even to the contrary. Often the true fruit upon the use of these means is not enjoyed until long after their use (John 5:41). "They that wait upon the LORD shall renew their strength; they shall mount up with wings as eagles" (Isa. 40:31). Coming from the Lord's Table, you may say what you have not received, but not that you shall never receive. As someone has said, it is fitting that the giver rather than the receiver will determine the time when He is pleased to bestow His gifts.

2. when, not perceiving any immediate joy upon partaking of the Lord's Supper, some postpone any reflection upon the same and permit it to fade from memory, thereby permitting all their sacramental zeal and disposition to remain inside the church doors. This is a common error, proceeding from ignorance of what we have previously addressed. If only it were understood that the Lord can render the Lord's Supper fruitful to our soul after its administration, one would not be so inclined to forget about it so quickly. However, having begun this spiritual work during the time of preparation, and having continued therein even before being fully engaged, the soul by way of reflection should then be all the more active to extract a measure of joy from this spiritual work. If one medication does not immediately yield results, the physician often supplements it with another, and in the end the benefit is obtained. Often a spice will not immediately give forth its scent when we take it into our hands, but it will ultimately yield its refreshing aroma if we repeatedly touch it. We must do likewise in regard to the Lord's Supper, and although there are no immediate results, we are to persevere and trust God's promise that our labor will not always be in vain in the Lord (1 Cor. 15:58).

Proposition #8: It is possible that a true Christian can sometimes be completely bereft of any spiritual joy proceeding from the Lord's Supper, and yet he receives and enjoys this Supper with genuine fruit.

The reason for this is that this joy is neither an essential component of one's partaking of the Lord's Supper, nor is such joy promised in an absolute sense but rather as a conditional promise.

Another reason is that in addition to such joy, the Lord's Supper yields many other fruits. In many cases it can yield more rather than less fruit to the soul, fruits such as humility, love, zeal, and others. We will subsequently speak of these fruits.

It can therefore be concluded once more how grievous an error it is

1. that some judge all Lord's Supper celebrations in which they did not enjoy comfort or joy as being useless and fruitless. They did attend, they confess, entirely without profit, using the argument

that they attended as stocks and blocks, and were barren and dull as they partook; they also confess that they departed from the table in that condition. It can nevertheless be that a lawful partaking of the Lord's Supper was not accompanied with such joy, and yet the soul will greatly benefit from such partaking even though she feels herself deprived at that moment from such sensible enjoyment. Though it is indeed true that all other fruitful stirrings of the heart constitute a large measure of the soul's taste and sweetness of this joy during the Lord's Supper, it does not mean that it loses its efficacy entirely, although for a season this delight is not experienced.

2. considering that there are others who not only render a particular attendance at the Lord's Supper suspect but who occasionally view their entire spiritual state as being suspect. Such ones frequently view themselves as entirely void of grace, because they generally partake of the Lord's Supper with such a lack of feeling and joy; this is something that has already gone on for quite a length of time. This would suggest that comfort rather than sanctifying grace constitutes conversion and that the Lord's Supper yields no other fruitfulness than only this spiritual joy. We have, however, already proven and concluded the contrary. Though it is true that consistent barrenness regarding such powerful and lively exercises cannot be reconciled with the new birth, such a conclusion is sometimes made too quickly. The fact is that both can very well co-exist. This is especially true when such barrenness is particularly defined as an absence of comfort and delight in regard to the Lord's Supper (as can be observed here and there), and not as a general lack of all holy and sanctifying motions regarding all spiritual exercises. Yes, we would even dare to add, believing it to be truly founded upon God's Word, that one who is truly born again can for a considerable period of time not only use and observe the Lord's Supper without tasting or perceiving any delight and sweetness in the same, but this can also be true for all other spiritual exercises—all the while retaining a painful sense of one's insensibility (Isa. 63:17; 64:5, 7; Ps. 119:25; Song 5:3, 6).

This concludes the first portion of the matter we had proposed to consider.

CHAPTER
2

I will now set before you the means and directions that not only will enable you to partake of the Lord's Supper with some fruit, but also, and especially, with joy and comfort. In this regard, some things are to be avoided and others to be practiced.

Regarding that which is to be avoided, we counsel you,

First, not to focus too much on the external aspects of the Lord's Supper, such as, for instance, the bread, the wine, the breaking of the bread, the act of eating and drinking, etc., or whatever else one is accustomed to do at that occasion. You might then be inclined to consider them to be the primary causes from which you would expect and anticipate your spiritual joy. You may, however, use them as means to that end. And you should focus all your attention and senses on them, without letting your eyes flit back and forth as some very foolishly do; but when you do, you are to do so without ending or resting in them. Rather, you should look to God by means of them, supplicating for and expecting your joy from Him alone who is the sole fountain of joy. Otherwise, if you do not look beyond the outward things, you will become either popish in considering a little piece of bread and a sip of wine to be your God, or will become Lutheran by seeking Christ, the consolation of Israel, where He is not to be found. Or you may degenerate to another form of shameful idolatry, wanting to ascribe to mere creatures a work that can only be ascribed to the God of heaven, and thereby you will bypass the fountain of living waters, hewing out "cisterns, broken cisterns, that can hold no water" (Jer. 2:13).[1] You are thus to set aside any notion that you will obtain this joy in a manner that you may have imagined. In fact, if you were thus able to derive joy from the Lord's Supper, it would follow irrefutably that all, including yourself, who use the external signs would experience this joy as much as you would, even if they were but dogs and swine. Then they would in reality become partakers of this joy as much as you would.

Second, you are not to trust in and rest upon the quality and worthiness of your preparation. Many err grievously in this regard. They view their preparation not only as a means whereby their souls are rendered more fit to experience this spiritual joy, but also as a basis for and reason why God should bestow this joy upon them in a more abundant and sure manner. For this reason, God will often not give them a greater measure of this joy (Luke 18:12–13). He rather denies and withholds it because He perceives that as a result of such inclinations they will no longer consider His sovereign love as the root of this joy, but rather look for this joy to some extent within themselves. This explains why it frequently happens that many troubled souls who have prepared themselves but little and who yet look entirely outside of themselves and expect it from Christ alone derive more comfort from the Lord's Supper than many who assume they have prepared themselves well and are therefore fit to receive this joy. Having said this, however, we do not wish to dissuade Christians from preparing themselves for the Lord's Supper as well as they possibly may be able. Rather, I wish to admonish them not to put their trust in their preparation, as the flesh often does so in a most subtle manner. They thereby defile their preparation, persuading themselves that joy will follow upon their actions, and they fail to be greatly ashamed about their brazenness. No preparation will achieve anything with God for its own sake, but it is only in the name of Christ that our preparation can be presented before God.

---

1. The text of the Dutch edition erroneously identifies the text as Jer. 11:13.

Third, if you are very despondent and leaning toward melancholy, and you proceed to partake of the Lord's Supper, see to it that you do not dwell on the disturbing and unsettling thoughts regarding your sins and failures. To you who are in a state of despondency, we say that we do not wish to apply this rule categorically, as if they who partake of the Lord's Supper should refrain from reflecting upon their sins. On the contrary! We believe that if someone comes to the Lord's Table in a somewhat sluggish and dull frame of mind, he must make a special effort to cause his dull heart to be broken so that the balm of grace may be all the more effective (Matt. 12:20). Nevertheless, concerning you who are of a melancholy and weak disposition, we believe that now, namely, the time of preparation for the Lord's Supper, is not the time to prune and carve even more, but rather that you should solely pursue the healing and refreshing of your soul. The reason why you so frequently leave the Lord's Table without fruit and joy is because you have been wrongly engaged, having focused more on your sins and abominations than on the grace of Jesus Christ. Such melancholy reflections will so oppress you and engulf your heart that the sunshine of God's comfort cannot penetrate. The best way for you and all that are of a similar disposition is but to cast your souls, as wounded and broken as they may be, before the cross of Christ, longing and craving for the sweet efficacy of His healing blood. Do so before you inflict new wounds in your soul.

You may say, "This would all be true if first I would have been sufficiently contrite and brokenhearted."

My reply is that it is not easy to determine the appropriate measure of such brokenheartedness. However, it is deep enough to be considered upright if

1. it is unrestricted, that is, if it has such an effect on your heart that you will never be able to conclude it is in proportion to your sins.

2. it truly humbles you and thus drives you outside of yourself to Christ.

3. it absolutely and unconditionally causes you to acknowledge your sins as being the cause of all this and if with your whole heart you desire to refrain from and to flee from them (2 Cor. 7:10).

Fourth, you are not to think lightly of this spiritual joy. Even among healthy believers there are those who have but little understanding of this. They repeatedly speak of nothing other than mortification, self-denial, the practice of various virtues, or about sanctifying grace in general. They would be inclined almost to sacrifice body and soul for it and to do very little to obtain this comforting grace. Often it does not matter much to them if they never would experience this joy as long as they may have these other graces. They appear to be well-intentioned; that is, they desire more and more to pursue that by which they can glorify God rather than something that would yield them peace and joy. However, unknowingly they make a serious error, an error that is often very subtle. Since, however, this affects even the best among the godly, we cannot pass it by silently. The soul's objective ought not only be that she esteems and seeks this spiritual joy, but also that she should stimulate it to the highest degree. This joy is an eminently blessed means to increase and stir up sanctifying grace (Neh. 8:10). And indeed, what fruit can you extract from underrating such a worthy and heavenly matter, other than that you thereby grieve the Holy Spirit, whose name and office encompass both comfort and sanctification? This will make you so vulnerable to grievous temptations to which joyless souls are more prone than joyful souls. God, who will not be disregarded, will then have cause at the Lord's Supper and other religious exercises to shut off His fountain of comfort and to make you suffer from this most when you can least afford it. You will undoubtedly have experienced that such a disregard for the joy of the Lord's Supper will generally cause your other related spiritual exercises, such as longing, exercising faith, supplicating, etc., also to decline and wilt.

These are the things you ought to avoid. The things you ought to practice, however, are the following:

First, learn to take careful notice of the excellence and preeminence of the Lord's Supper. A lack of knowledge regarding a matter prevents us from having a desire for it, and such a lack of desire for it will result in a lack of joy regarding it. To partake of the Lord's Supper is not, as the world views it, a work of little value, but rather in multiple ways it is an excellent work—and yes, even divine. It is the communion of the body and blood of Christ; it is the table of the Lord; and it is a vivid and divine portrayal of the Savior's suffering, dying, being broken, and being eaten and drunk for those who were His murderers. It is a display of the incomprehensible God whom the heavens and the earth cannot contain but who resides in the humble abode of the human heart; it is the king of kings being present among beggars; it is a prominent master being in the presence of insignificant slaves; and yes, it is the light of lights dwelling among those who are by nature nothing but darkness. And then there are other innumerable matters of excellence, regarding some of which we will subsequently say a bit more. Diligently commit your heart to this and you will experience that it will be filled with much comfort and sweetness. "Oh how great is your goodness, which you have laid up for them that fear you; which you have prepared for them that trust in you before the sons of men!" (Ps. 30:19).[2]

Second, when seated at the table, engage your faith in a lively and vigorous manner. Christ is the essence of this spiritual joy, and the ability to experience its delight proceeds from Christ. Such joy must therefore be extracted from Him by faith, for as we believe, we will rejoice with joy unspeakable (1 Peter 1:8). The comfort that is to be obtained in this way is spiritual, and one must therefore feed upon it with a spiritual mouth; and this mouth is faith alone.

Question: How shall I initiate the exercise of my faith in this regard?
Answer: Assure yourself

---

2. The text of the Dutch edition erroneously identifies the text as Ps. 31:10.

1. that not only is the Lord's Supper God's ordinance, but that at the appointed time you are also using it lawfully and according to His ordinance.

2. that in the way of His own ordinance, He will manifest Himself efficaciously to your heart so that it will yield the desired spiritual comfort and joy or such other fruits as He deems to be in your best interest at the time.

3. that whatever the minister does and says at the table is not merely him acting and speaking, but that it truly is the Lord Jesus Himself who through him presents and distributes His blessed body for spiritual consumption; and he adds this glorious promise, "Take, eat, this is my body which is broken for you; do this in remembrance of me, etc." (1 Cor. 11:24–25).[3]

4. that you are to cast your soul upon this divine promise alone and let your faith take this to be its one and only resting place. And let this not be contingent upon the degree of worthiness and fitness you find within yourself. "Let him that is athirst come. And whosoever will, let him take the water of life freely" (Rev. 22:17); "Come, buy wine and milk without money and without price" (Isa. 55:1).

5. that not only are you to consider the partaking of a particular Lord's Supper in general as a sign and seal of the forgiveness of all your sins, but also specifically of those sins and failures that perhaps at the moment of your partaking (albeit against your will) may have troubled and ensnared you: dullness of heart, lack of reverence, fearfulness, wandering thoughts, etc. Experience teaches that if the exercise of faith focuses not specifically on them, but rather only on sin in general, some souls will not only partake of the Lord's Supper with a sense of condemnation—I know not why, but it will affect many other spiritual exercises as well! The result will be that they engage in them not only without joy, but also entirely without fruit.

---

3. The text of the Dutch edition erroneously identifies the text as 1 Cor. 10:16–17.

Third, try as much as possible to deny and to set aside your own pleasure in the partaking of the Lord's Supper. Do this not only in regard to a certain measure of joy, of which we have spoken in the preceding, but also in regard to all that transpires at the Lord's Table.

Also in this regard, it is true that many souls obstinately insist upon a given measure of humility, spirituality, faith, attentiveness, etc., having determined themselves that they would partake of a given Lord's Supper in such a frame (Acts 21:14). If this fails to materialize for them, they often leave the Lord's Table dissatisfied and perplexed (Matt. 26:39). Nevertheless, we hereby maintain that one should wholeheartedly desire to partake of the Lord's Supper in a good spiritual frame and strive for this to the utmost of his ability. It should indeed be your concern that it be so (1 Sam. 3:18). However, if God the Lord would be pleased to let things turn out differently after you have done your part, you are then to be somewhat more flexible and indifferent; yes, be content with that which the Lord is pleased to give you and to approve of it at that particular moment. In all things, it is a steadfast rule that the more willing we are to suffer for the Lord's sake, the more inclined He will be to give us our desire. If, therefore, it is your desire to derive comfort and joy from the Lord's Supper, then use the appointed means to this end and allow the Lord to do as He pleases. You are to learn from this that if He is pleased not to give this to you, then you are to strive to find your delight even in the fact that you are missing it. It will then be all the more likely that you will receive it.

Question: Is it possible to be satisfied when I must deal with insensitivity, lack of reverence, drowsiness, etc.? And am I not often overcome by all these deficiencies when I am seated at the table?

Answer: Not at all, but you are to wrestle and struggle against these deficiencies with all your might. At the same time, however, you are to be satisfied and submissive under the all-wise government of God whereby He purposes that precisely at such a moment you should be of such a disposition. You are, however, not to be resigned to your deficiencies, for they are sinful and cannot be the foundation of any true satisfaction. Though such a disposition in and of itself is sinful and evil and consequently gives you grief, it is overruled by His government. This providential arrangement as such is therefore always good and holy and a sufficient ground to oblige you to submit. Such a measure of self-denial is great indeed, and yet needful. This is particularly true since failure to have it will often grievously deprive the most eminent of souls of all their comfort regarding the Lord's Supper.

Fourth, whatever the motions of your heart might be during the Lord's Supper, let them be what they are and learn to focus on something good and beneficial for your soul. The reason why you often depart uncomforted from the Lord's Supper is that you consider these stirrings of your corrupt flesh, of which you perhaps become aware contrary to your intentions, only as to their external effect and without being able to detect any fruit for yourself. This is an error, for God can so order it that even as you engage in spiritual activity, that which is most evil and may even occur unexpectedly can yield exceptional benefit for you.

Often you think, "I have indeed attended the Lord's Supper. However, I was so carnal, hard-hearted, inattentive, etc. What comfort can I derive from it?" Your deficiencies as such can yield none. But there will be some insofar as the Lord causes it to be to your advantage. For this ill frame of heart, though in and of itself it can yield no satisfaction to you, can nevertheless, insofar as it is seen and experienced by you, cause you to humble yourself more, cause you to forsake yourself, and cause you to take refuge in Christ. It will thus prompt you to be more careful and spiritual in your preparation.

What do you think? Is this not applicable to all of us? Furthermore, is this not in some measure enough (even if there was nothing else) to stir up and ignite in you some measure of holy joy? This is all the more evident when considering that these effects of your deficiencies can simultaneously be indications that you truly are a partaker of Christ. It is He who is the preeminent and essential substance of all genuine spiritual joy.

Fifth, learn to value and esteem even the external use of the Lord's Supper, even though at that moment you do so without tasting any sweetness. It is not good if we exclusively focus on the externals, but it is also not good to consider them to be of no value. You may often be of the opinion that by having partaken of the bread and wine, you have done nothing else but to have eaten and drunk damnation to yourself, since you did it in such an external and fleshly manner and did so without detecting any desire or sweetness. This, in turn, is the cause that at such occasions you will often feel more distraught and sorrowful than joyful. This is all due to your own lack of understanding and erroneous thinking. Although we do not wish in any way either to justify or excuse your lack of desire regarding such important exercises, and although we heartily lament your case if the Lord is pleased to lead you in such a way, you must for that reason alone not abandon your hope of experiencing joy at the Lord's Supper. One can nevertheless partake in a manner pleasing to God and thus also profitably, even though it is often done without any spiritual desire, as long as that is present of which I will speak shortly.

People who suffer from a cold derive a great deal of benefit from their food that they generally consume without having any smell or taste. And thus, though for a season you may lack any sensible sweetness in your holy exercises, we are certain that you nevertheless concur wholeheartedly in this: that such spiritual exercises are worthy of being engaged in with the greatest desire and delight in the world. This will be true if you truly fear the Lord! This will happen when you are wholeheartedly sighing and wishing that you might perform them in that fashion. That, in and of itself, qualifies as delight and desire. Even if the feeling of it is absent, it is there in principle and as to the root of the matter.

We must here, of necessity, add the following: to partake of the Lord's Supper, aside from it being God's institution, is also a matter of duty and holy obedience, and is to be observed in spite of your sorrow over the deficiencies that accompany your partaking. You therefore know that although you could not partake with delight and desire, you may not think lightly of your partaking. In fact, the performance of a duty is truly most glorious when it is divorced from the personal delight of the one who practices it and when he continues to do so exclusively for its own sake and for the glory of the one who commands it. If you were perhaps to taste such sweetness and delight in the Lord's Supper as you would desire, you would readily desire it more for its sensual delight than in response to God's command. You would consequently use it perhaps more out of love for yourself rather than focusing upon the duty.

If, therefore, you feel yourself to be so desireless, it is perhaps God's intent thereby to test you as to what you are willing to do and take in hand when prompted by His command alone. He may be prompting you apart from and even contrary to your own desire and profit. If, then, you do not sense anything during the Lord's Supper, you ought nevertheless to rejoice (therefore, do so!) in the fact that you have at least received this of the Lord: that you have been able and willing to observe His ordinance without any joy for yourself. Such obedience, which is very spiritual and pure, will by no means lose its reward. In fact, there is even the clear promise of obtaining this spiritual joy: "He that has my commandments and keeps them, he it is that loves me; and he that loves me shall be loved of my Father, and I will love him and will manifest myself to him" (John 14:21).

Sixth, we must learn not to seek this spiritual joy in the Lord's Supper for its own sake. Rather, we must learn that this joy may be a means to bring forth more holiness and bring us nearer to God. Otherwise you may have some counterfeit peace; but this renders to God little or no honor. You know, however, that it is for the sake of His glory that He bestows all blessings upon His children. "I will run the way of your commandments when you enlarge my heart" (Ps. 119:32). If this joy does not sanctify you, it will puff you up and make you careless. It will leave as its residue nothing but harm and grief for you, and it will cause God to be put to shame and be dishonored.

Therefore, see to it that you do not pursue spiritual joy in the wrong way, for not all seekers shall here become finders. Only they will become finders who, as in all other matters, seek least for themselves and most for Christ. It would undoubtedly be nothing but a sort of spiritual sensuality in you if you were to elevate your own pleasure as essential for spiritual strengthening—as if that were to be the preeminent purpose of your partaking of the Lord's Supper.

Solomon says that they who eat in due season will eat for strength and not for drunkenness (Eccl. 10:17). We will soon address this more extensively.

CHAPTER
3

We will now proceed with our third objective: to address the objections, or rather, the difficulties that at times trouble and distress God's children regarding the absence of this spiritual joy.

Objection #1: Not only do I fail to derive any joy from the Lord's Supper, but often I leave this supper far more distraught and unsettled than before I came.

Answer: 1. This is not uncommon, particularly if you are a weak Christian or if the disposition of your soul is weak at that given moment. The condition of such people will generally be similar to that of a weak body that shortly after a meal will feel worse than before, and nevertheless will derive strength from the meal.

2. In partaking of the Lord's Supper, you have drawn nearer to Christ, the light of the world. However, the nearer you draw to this light, the clearer you will perceive your sins. Your condition can possibly be caused by your faith being somewhat inactive, also causing you to be more distraught.

3. Perhaps it is God's intent that by your being distraught and unsettled, He will compensate for and/or perfect that which, as you complained, was lacking in your preparation.

4. He does not give each of His children the same measure of fruit at each celebration of the Lord's Supper, but to everyone He

gives according to what He knows them to be most in need of in their present spiritual condition. If, therefore, you are more sorrowful than joyful, this is undoubtedly because it will presently be more beneficial for you to be somewhat cast down rather than to be lifted up.

5. It is not uncommon for God to allow notable distress to precede heavenly joy, similar to a downpour that precedes the sunshine. Christ has said, "You shall be sorrowful, but your sorrow shall be turned into joy."[1]

Objection #2: Yes, but I fear that the fault is mine and that I did not prepare myself as well as I should have, etc., and therefore I cannot find any comfort.

Answer: 1. Search very diligently whether you yourself are the cause of this or if the cause is otherwise.

2. However, do not jump to conclusions. If you cannot find sufficient proof within yourself that you are at fault, it will impact your spiritual joy very negatively by imagining yourself to be at fault when in reality this is not so.

3. By no means deem all imperfect preparation to be insincere and deficient.

4. If there truly was some deficiency in your preparation, then do not fixate on it too long, but rather, humble yourself before God with regard to this matter, come before Him believing in the atoning blood of Christ, and conduct yourself better in the future.

5. Consider also that God, though very ready to grant you such joy, may nevertheless withhold it from you. As was mentioned earlier, He may do this because you are resting in this joy, because He wants to teach you that He is not obligated to grant what you are seeking, or because He wants you to feel that you are not always as ready to serve Him as He is ready to be served by you.

---

1. John 16:20.

Objection #3: I see that others find such joy in the Lord's Supper. O Lord, why can I also not have such joy?

Answer: 1. Be not envious of someone else's joy, but, as much as possible, seek to emulate them, and "Rejoice with them that do rejoice."[2]

2. Not all who display such joy are truly joyful, for the hypocrites will frequently display a great deal of bravado.

3. It could also be that they belong to the godly, and you are only observing their outward conduct. They conduct themselves as such so that you would not become even more dejected, or because they do not want religion in general or this memorable event to be maligned. However, they may also have inner turmoil and sorrow in their hearts that you cannot observe.

4. If they are genuinely joyful, then consider that every Christian has his own season of joy. For some that may be true now, and perhaps this was so for you at another time when others lacked such joy. We are to "remember the years of the right hand of the Most High" (Ps. 77:10).

Objection #4: I would be able to thank and glorify God far better if I could also experience such joy.

Answer: 1. There is much reason for gratitude that you are so desirous to be more grateful.

2. If you are without spiritual joy, you may be lacking the special means and motives to glorify God, but that does not mean that there is neither substance nor cause to glorify Him.

3. The real issue here is what it means to glorify Him in the most spiritual manner. Truly, if you had a great deal of this joy, you might be motivated more by this joy and less motivated by grace, more by the sweetness drawn from Christ than by the Lord Christ Himself. You need to understand, however, that the latter is ten times more spiritual than the former.

---

2. Rom. 12:15.

Objection #5: I do derive some spiritual joy from the Lord's Supper, but it is so short-lived and fleeting that I almost do not know what to make of it.

Answer: 1. This is not surprising nor uncommon, but rather something most delightful and precious. God deals with His children as wise parents deal with their children. They occasionally will give them some delicacies, but they are not at all inclined to give them every day or for any lengthy period of time.

2. The Lord also knows what is best for His children. We are naturally and easily inclined to be excessively attracted to such sweetness and spiritual dispositions, so that we become careless and drowsy, or we become too sensitive and spoiled. It is not good when we eat too much honey. God therefore readily withdraws His hand, and thereby abuse is prevented.

3. This spiritual joy can also be viewed in a twofold manner. Such joy can be the result of God's special speaking and the comforting stirring of the souls of His children, though this is not the common way. He sometimes and immediately will say to their souls, "I am your salvation" (Ps. 35:3; see also Eph. 1:13 and Ps. 4:6), and, "I am yours and you are mine."[3] Or, their joy will be in proportion to seeing—at least to the degree that He grants reflection upon it—that those graces identified in His Word as being signs and proofs that they are His are truly found in them (2 Peter 1:6). We believe that the former is generally very brief and often like a flash of lightning. The latter joy, however, though it can be intertwined with darkness, is nevertheless more stable and of longer duration. The godly may and should therefore primarily seek and take note of this, regardless of whether the former joy has vanished or lasts for a considerable time.

4. Perhaps you do not value your joy experienced at the Lord's Supper sufficiently, and it therefore vanishes all the more quickly. Or, when you begin to perceive a measure of such comfort, you

---

3. Isa. 43:1.

will be quite readily inclined to set aside the renewed and daily exercise of your faith, your labor of love, and the disciplined use of the ordinary means of grace. These are, nevertheless, the things whereby such joy must be nourished and sustained. Therefore, seek to improve your conduct in the future in this regard, and observe whether you retain this joy for a longer period of time.

5. And though it may readily diminish, you must learn not to measure its extended value merely by the period of time you feel this joy, but also by the extended and powerful impression it makes upon you (Ps. 73:28). Then you will be enabled to cleave to God to the utmost of your ability, to cleave to the God whose goodness you have tasted for such a brief period of time.

Objection #6: I feel so pressured to abstain from the Lord's Supper entirely because I perceive that my partaking always appears to be in vain.

Answer: 1. This is a device of the devil, and you must strive against lending him your ear. He is displeased with your peace and joy, and he therefore seeks to wrest from you those means that are subservient to it. If you completely were to cease nourishing your body, this would for some time weaken you more than it would strengthen you.

2. Are you saying that your partaking of the Lord's Supper is in vain when you receive no comfort at all from it? Are there no other fruits except this one? We believe there are, and this will soon become evident.

3. If you were to desist completely from partaking of the Lord's Supper, would you enjoy more comfort and joy? Would you not deprive yourself completely of all hope? What would you have gained?

Additional Objection: At least I could not eat and drink judgment to myself.

Answer: If you partake of the Lord's Supper, seeking your salvation in Christ alone and with true humility of heart, albeit without experiencing any feeling or joy, you will not be eating judgment to yourself. In fact, if such is your disposition, and you do not partake, you will by renewal make your judgment all the heavier. As long as you continue with this neglect, you will not be able to assure yourself that you have been delivered from this condemnation.

Part II:
On Sanctification

CHAPTER
4

⁎

Hopefully I have achieved my objective by sufficiently addressing the pathway one is to pursue in deriving comfort and spiritual joy from the Lord's Supper. It now follows that we also proceed to say something about the manner in which sanctification can be stimulated by partaking of the Lord's Supper. I can perhaps be somewhat briefer than in the preceding section, since various matters already addressed may be useful here as well. And there are other matters from which we can glean at least as much instruction regarding this subject as are found in part one.

It is common knowledge that sanctification has two branches. It either focuses on the lamenting, hating, and fleeing from evil, or on the longing for and seeking of that which is good. Partaking of the Lord's Supper can wonderfully influence the stimulation of both aspects of sanctification. By God's grace, I shall use general propositions to demonstrate this in a variety of ways. I will also show you how to make use of them by identifying several special and noteworthy characteristics of the Lord's Supper.

Proposition #1: To partake of the Lord's Supper is a work of extraordinary necessity. This necessity is twofold: 1) It is a duty required by God; 2) It is a suitable and moral means to stimulate the grace of sanctification in us (Matt. 26:1; 1 Cor. 10:16–17; 11:24).

This identifies the error of those who

1. believe that it is a matter of indifference to partake of the Lord's Supper and that we are at liberty either to partake or to abstain. So many are entirely unconcerned about this, considering that whoever partakes does well but that it is also not a grievous sin to abstain. These continually devise their excuses and argue with those that exhort them to partake. Regretfully, such people err seriously. It is praiseworthy that those who may partake of the Lord's Supper do indeed partake, but it is equally true that those who abstain are guilty of a great sin. It is Christ who commands us to partake, as He did on the threshold of His last sufferings, when He attached a special promise to this command. Therefore, woe to that person who will not submit to His express will! This is particularly true when considering that Christ did not give this command for His own sake or to His own advantage. He rather gave it for our benefit, because it is His desire to provide a weak person with a powerful means to live a more joyful and holier life. Therefore, they that are neglectful in this regard wrong both God and themselves. God is offended by the neglect of His command, and the believer sins against God by depriving himself of such a glorious means that can be so suitable to promote godliness and happiness.

2. do indeed partake of the Lord's Supper, but do so purely as a duty and without considering it as a means to advance in sanctification. This is confirmed by the fact that they generally, as we have already mentioned, are satisfied with the simple enjoyment of this meal. They believe that they have fulfilled their duty by having enjoyed the Lord's Supper, and that therefore all is well. If, however, they were to view their partaking as a means for spiritual growth, they would certainly also look for the fruit proceeding from the use of this means.

Christians, how remiss we are in this regard! How rarely it happens that, upon having partaken of the Lord's Supper, we search our hearts regarding the effects and their outworking of the matter at hand. Is there anyone who makes a concerted effort to take personal inventory from time to time, and thus investigates whether the frequent partaking of the Lord's Supper has yielded either spiritual improvement or decline (Mic. 7:7–8)? Who is troubled by the fact that he detects no improvement? Or, who glorifies God when he perceives that he has benefited from the same? Truly, even the best among the godly must be ashamed that they never have truly understood this proposition or that they all too frequently have been negligent. Who would plant a vineyard without investigating the fruit it produces? Who would take medication without observing its effect? Who would use a means unto sanctification, which the Lord's Supper is, without discerning the benefits derived from it?

Proposition #2: The Lord's Supper is an excellent, glorious, and heavenly matter, as we have previously demonstrated. Its author is heavenly; the matter symbolized is heavenly; the partakers are heavenly; the promises are heavenly; and the fruits are heavenly. Yes, everything is heavenly!

Therefore, they err grievously

1. who greatly minimize this supper; who readily neglect its use; and who often abstain for the least defilement from the world, for the slightest obstacle, for an unpleasant encounter, or even for uttering harsh words. Such persons are truly blind and have never correctly understood what a glorious work it is to partake. They are ignorant of God's gift and do not know what it means to eat with God—yes, even to feed upon God Himself, and to receive Him in the heart by faith. If they had but eyes to see and hearts to understand this gift, they would rather incline toward refraining from eating, drinking, sleeping, and all the pleasures of the world than, upon having been invited to this plentiful meal, to abstain or to use frivolous excuses for not partaking without there being any urgent reason to do so. O perverted man of this world! If Satan holds before you some dust of the earth, a shadow of insignificant human honor, and a handful of foolish and numbing pleasures, you eagerly yearn for this and seize upon this without anyone being able to stop you. However, when God invites and calls you—yes, when He beseeches you to come to His table and to be His guest—so that by the use of these holy signs and seals you will receive the most enduring benefits, what else could then

be more necessary and profitable than this? Oh, Lord, deliver us from such a world of foolishness!

2. who are so ungrateful for such heavenly grace. Oh, children of God, this also reveals your ignorance of the glorious substance you may enjoy when you partake of the Lord's Supper. When at times you complain about a lack of temporal bread, behold this heavenly bread! What if you were banished from the table of the rich? Behold, then, a spiritual and heavenly meal that is prepared for you—yes, especially for you who are rich in faith and poor in this world's goods. Here the poor may glory in their riches. Yes, whoever you may be, whether poor or rich, mourn the fact that you have not sufficiently mourned your ingratitude. Whether you are ill, despised, or uncomforted, behold this joyous table prepared for you in heaven and set before you here on earth. Consider the host, the food, the drink, and your fellow guests. Let them all stir you up to sanctify you and to redeem you. Where is your acknowledgment, your praise, and your heavenly conversation, whereby the world may see that you have not been nourished by its insignificant husks but rather with heavenly nourishment?

Proposition #3: The Lord's Supper does not consist of elaborate procedures, but rather is a very simple transaction.

Consider all the accessories of this institution: they are visible, tangible, tasteful, and common things. There is no elaborate slaying of a lamb at any specific time or place—a lamb that is entirely free of blemish or of a specific age, or which is to be eaten with certain sauces as was done at the Passover. Instead, there is simply bread and common wine, items that are as familiar to us as our daily food.

It will therefore be evident that they err

1. who make such an elaborate and outward show when they come to the Lord's Table. There are those who, because of their deplorable garment and/or sober clothing, will abstain. And there are those who deem it to be a privilege that they can appear there all spruced up and decorated. Both are guilty of an entirely wrong

and dishonoring assessment of the edifying simplicity of this holy institution. Was Christ at all concerned about the garments of His apostles when He sat with them at the table? Did He reject them because they were too modest, or did He praise them because of their ornaments? He did neither of the two! God looks at the heart and not at our clothing. That which is most simple pleases Him most. God is a Spirit, and therefore, as long as there is spiritual adornment, He frequently despises and even abhors that which is external. Yes, it would amount to accusing Him of foolishness if He were to insist on a celebration with so much external ado, since He instituted it with such exceptional simplicity.

2. who despise the Lord's Table because of such simplicity of arrangement. "It only consists of a piece of bread and a little wine," so they say. What efficacy can there be in this, and what effect can this have? How misguided and arrogant are such people who would prescribe to the God of heaven whether He should graciously strengthen the souls of His children by either simple or elaborate means! They thereby reveal that they have but a carnal mind, seeking the efficacy of the Lord's Supper only in its external accessories. And indeed, if the externals were to be the essence of the matter, there would be very little by which to form any opinion. However, it is neither merely bread and wine, nor the few ceremonial actions such as taking, breaking, and pouring, whereby souls are strengthened and sanctified. Rather, it is God's Spirit and the power of Christ, on the basis of the divine institution and promise, that accompany the use of these insignificant and simple objects. It is immaterial to God whether He helps by much or by little, whether He uses some earthly mire, or speaks but a word, or makes but a gesture. All the means will be insufficient to make the blind to see, to heal the sick, or to create even the entire world if they are not accompanied by His power.

Proposition #4: The partaking of the Lord's Supper itself is neither complicated nor difficult, but rather, it is something that can be very easily observed.

It is not like the sacrament of circumcision, which was accompanied with much pain and grief. It involves no loss of either time or money, and as far as external matters are concerned, it can be very easily and readily partaken.

Extenuating Argument: Yes, but the external use of this sacrament is not sufficient. It must also be used in a spiritual fashion, which is something that involves so much more!

Answer: 1. It is true that an external use of this sacrament is insufficient. However, it is commendable when a given aspect of our religious exercises is not too complicated as to its externals.

2. The spiritual dimension of the Lord's Supper is also not burdensome for the converted, who alone may partake, when they consider that God grants His helping and sustaining grace. "I can do all things through Christ who strengthens me" (Phil. 4:13; see also Matt. 11:29 and 1 John 5:3). This is true with reference to the Lord's Supper as well as all other matters.

From this it can be concluded

1. how misguided such persons are who, by imagining it to be difficult and problematic, allow themselves to be discouraged from engaging in this holy activity. "It is such a burden, such a burden," so they cry, "and it is not easy to begin with it and even more difficult to proceed with it, etc." However, you are relying upon a foolish excuse! What is the difficulty about this, unless by your own fault you make it difficult? All you are to do is to eat a piece of bread and drink a sip of wine. This is as difficult as it was for Adam and Eve, who desired the forbidden fruit. Were there not heavier burdens in the Old Testament that neither we nor our fathers were able to bear? Consider the washings, the sacrifices, the feast days, and all the traveling to and from Jerusalem, etc. What millstones are hung around the necks of the poor papists! What bodily torture, what pilgrimages, what false mortification, and yes, what manifold distractions even regarding the Lord's Supper! The Lord Christ sets us free from all of these by the manner in which He instituted the Lord's Supper. Who would still claim that He is so

harsh, inconsiderate, and merciless, and that He demands such difficult work from us? For the unrepentant it is truly a burden. However, for them everything that even smacks of religion is a burden. Therefore, repent, and it shall become both spiritually and externally an easy task for you.

2. how foolish and irrational they are who for purely carnal convenience refuse to partake of the Lord's Supper, doing this especially because they would then have to break fully with sin and the world. They act as if the service of these ruthless tyrants would be easier and more tolerable than this lovely and sweet institution of Christ, who requires such reasonable things and who helps us carry the burdens He imposes upon us. He will even be satisfied with an inadequate performance if it is done in sincerity and with all our heart, and in the end He will bestow such a great reward upon such deficient service. However, Satan, sin, and the world impose their iron laws, which bring the hearts of men into such bondage that they are continually burdened by the requirement to obey them all. Whose life is more sour than they who must serve such lords as continually devise new customs and fashions with which they burden their slaves so severely that their subjects can have no inner peace unless they subscribe to them all?

Just ask a vain court attendant! She would be able to testify how much effort is involved to keep in step with all the extravagant ornaments that the arbitrary standards of the court prescribe. Is the government imposed by sin and Satan so gentle and easy that it causes some to believe that they ought to avoid the comforting yoke of the Lord's Supper? Poor people, you are as blind as moles, and you slavishly subject yourself to this world! Become wiser and no longer prefer hell above heaven, a funeral banquet above a joyous meal, and the service of the most cruel, ungodly, and ungrateful murderers above the command of Christ to eat a piece of bread in remembrance of Him.

Proposition #5: In and by the lawful use of the Lord's Supper, the sealing of grace will progress to its highest degree and will be certain and infallibly secure. (Matt. 26:26; 1 Cor. 10:16–17; Ps. 93:5).

It is therefore erroneous

1. that some, because they are so weak in the faith and have so little assurance of their salvation, at times abstain from partaking of the Lord's Supper. They dare not partake because they lack assurance. Instead, however, they should partake in order to attain such assurance. The Lord's Supper is the pledge or wedding ring whereby it pleases Christ to enlarge our hearts in a more powerful and lively manner. If we were always emotionally engaged and always steadfast in our walk, the Lord's Supper would not be needed. All the more reason for us to partake, for it is here that we most frequently fail. Who would refrain from eating because he is too weak? Precisely, then, one ought to eat in order to become stronger.

Extenuating Argument: But I may nevertheless not partake of the Lord's Supper unless I am assured of my adoption, conversion, etc., for one cannot partake fruitfully unless he is in possession of these things.

Answer: a. Such assurance exists in degrees. It is either more obscure or clearer. The latter is not always the case, but in some measure there will be the first.

b. There is an assurance of sense and an assurance of faith, a faith that cleaves to its object. Without the latter no one can rightly partake of the Lord's Supper, but one can do so without the assurance of sense.

c. There is an assurance of our inclination toward God. That must always be present. However, there is also the assurance of God's inclination toward us. And though this can be absent, it does not mean that we should abstain from the Lord's Supper. This is because our favorable inclination toward God is in and of itself sufficient evidence of God's inclination toward us, even though for a season we cannot perceive this connection.

2. when others are so suspicious of an assurance derived from the Lord's Supper, for they are of the opinion that this may not be relied upon too much. This manifests itself in the fact that many souls, however many times they may have partaken of the Lord's Supper, are nevertheless as uncertain and doubtful as before. Upon

the question why, in light of such sensible, visible, tangible, and delightful evidences, they are not more assured of God's grace, they frequently will reply that they do not dare to go. They could deceive themselves, for there are many who readily assure themselves and will yet be deceived in the end, etc.

By such reasoning, one truly brings dishonor upon the Lord's Supper and Him who instituted it. What sort of argument is this? Because there are those who deceive themselves, it does not mean that no one can rightfully assure himself. This is a popish sophistication! Since there are many who reassure themselves that they are wise even though they are not, must we then conclude that no one is capable of assuring himself that he is truly wise? The reason why many deceive themselves regarding their assurance is not because the Lord's Supper and its sealing function are suspect, but because they build their assurance on false foundations. Such false foundations are: 1) one's own imagination, 2) external blessings, 3) the magnitude of God's mercies without any regard to His justice, 4) the external use of the Lord's Supper, etc. We admit that such assurance is defective.

However, if one partakes of the Lord's Supper with a sanctified heart, leaning solely upon God's promise annexed to it, how can a person then deceive himself? Then God Himself would be deceiving us. I maintain that if someone partakes of the Lord's Supper lawfully, he may indeed assure himself that Christ and all His benefits are his portion, doing so as surely as the person himself is a man and as surely as God is God. It would indeed be possible that God should be no God, if upon promising His communion to someone, the contrary proved to be true.

Extenuating Argument: Yes, but the problem is this: Has God specifically promised His communion to me by means of the Lord's Supper? It is reasonable that the one to whom He has made this promise would assure himself upon His Word. However, has He made that promise to me?

Answer: He promises this to all true partakers of the Lord's Supper. If you are such a one, then why has He not promised it to you? Has He excluded you? Are you asking whether you are a true partaker? My response is that you are, because you are concerned whether you are. It is such concern, if it is genuine, which indicates that you ought to be absolutely convinced that you are one, for it is your heartfelt desire to be one of them. They who thus hunger and thirst to be the Lord's are truly His (Matt. 5:6; Isa. 55:1).

CHAPTER
5

Thus far we have considered general propositions regarding the Lord's Supper. This has enabled us to discern the many deficient views and misunderstandings regarding sanctification, and that they can only be identified and denounced in light of its distinctives.

The means whereby a godly life may be promoted are twofold: some pertain to sanctification in general, others pertain to some of its particular members or branches.

Regarding the first, the following needs to be observed:

1. The soul that is desirous to partake of the Lord's Supper should learn to take note of her special obligation toward an increase in sanctification. She not only must view this as an essential component of godliness, the practice of which will identify her as being one of the godly, but also as a renewal of a greater and stronger commitment to a greater and more abundant measure of godliness. For as often as you partake of the Lord's Supper, you thereby not only commit yourself to the exercise of new virtues, but you also stir up your soul to a more exact and steadfast commitment to what has been practiced heretofore. This is also true in regard to prayer. Even before you pray, you already are obliged to obey God in all things. If, however, you truly desire to be heard by God, then whenever you proceed to pray again, you must reaffirm your former commitment to heed God's commandments. For comprehended in all

these duties are explicit promises to obey the one from whom we desire to receive all good things.

It is undoubtedly a common occurrence that some, though they frequently partake of the Lord's Supper, neither grow in grace nor become holier. They are of the opinion that to partake of the Lord's Supper is but one of the things to which godliness obliges them, rather than that it is the Lord's Supper that obliges them to a greater measure of godliness. One reason for this may be that some neither give any thought nor take to heart that their commitment to holiness should be strengthened by means of the Lord's Supper. Worldly people often understand this connection very well, and therefore they do not wish to partake of the Lord's Supper simply because it obligates them to a more exact and holier life. We have stated earlier that this conclusion is true, but it should not be a reason for anyone to abstain.

In the meantime, it would be desirable for many professing Christians to obtain a firmer grasp of this, and it would make them much more vigilant in the use of the various means of grace. With God's blessing, a better and more conscientious use of these means would cause them to make considerable progress in sanctification.

2. The soul should also stimulate her hunger and thirst for the Lord's Supper. Food will never have a more strengthening effect than when consumed with delight. "Blessed are they which hunger and thirst after righteousness: for they shall be filled" (Matt. 5:6). This is according to God's own promise: "Open your mouth wide, and I will fill it" (Ps. 81:10b). Having said this, it should be noted that this hunger and thirst does not pertain so much to the external partaking of the Lord's Supper, except insomuch as it is a means whereby God is pleased to work the increase of grace in us, but primarily to a renewed and more intimate manifestation of the Lord Jesus to and in our hearts. It is Christ who is the power and wisdom of God (1 Cor. 1:24), and the One from whom all things proceed. It is He who by the power of His death mortifies the old and strengthens the new man. It is therefore an error of many troubled souls when at times, due to excessive despondency, they quench their appetite for the Lord's Supper to such an extent

that, instead of longing for it, they frequently stir up fear in their hearts toward it. When by and by they begin to think about it, they become increasingly troubled. How can the Lord's Supper then yield spiritual strength when, according to the testimony of such souls, they often feel that their partaking, if they do partake, is imposed upon them as it were against their wishes?

3. The soul, while exercised with the Lord's Supper, must continually come before the Lord with groanings, supplications, and extemporaneous prayers. In faith, she must cling to Him and not let Him go, except that He bless her. As stated earlier, her eyes must be fixed upon the minister, the bread, the wine, and all the ceremonial details of this event; and her ears must be attuned to the words of the institutional formula and promise. Meanwhile, a steady stream of supplications must ascend to heaven, saying, "O Lord, strengthen me; comfort me; sanctify me through this spiritual work; increase my faith," etc. Consider David's success in this regard: "In the day when I cried, you answered me and strengthened me with strength in my soul (Ps. 138:3). If, however, following the Lord's Supper it occasionally happens that you feel just as listless, weak, and without appropriate desires as you did beforehand, then consider: whether you have sufficiently cried to the Lord for His reviving power; whether during the Lord's Supper you have been engaged in prayer with sighing and crying to Him as you ought to have been; and whether your partaking as such (*opus operatum*) cannot yield a blessing. The minister cannot give it to you, and you cannot give it to yourself. God must grant the blessing, and He is also willing to do so, but not unless we frequently and earnestly supplicate Him for it (Ps. 85:3).

4. The soul must often bring to mind her partaking of the Lord's Supper, and then specifically what God has therein bestowed upon her and what she, in return, has promised Him. All too readily we forget what has been good, and all too easily we are weary of reflecting on such matters. This is to be regretted, for by refreshing our memories regarding these matters, our sanctification would thereby be greatly advanced. If only we would reflect the next

morning on our partaking of the Lord's Supper as well as the commitment to which we have thereby obliged our souls! I doubt not but that in so doing not only would we be kept from many offenses, but we would be stimulated toward much that is good. Daily we think about our clothes, our eating and drinking, the labor of our hands, our artistic accomplishments, etc. However, all of this pertains only to our bodies. Why, then, do we not equally reflect upon the Lord's Supper, since it so greatly benefits our souls? O, what corrupt vessels we are! Even our memories are torn and frayed on all sides, so that especially those things that are good, beneficial, and edifying, instead of being retained, are permitted to leak out on all sides. However, when it comes to all evil things, such as our vices and resentment regarding inflicted injuries, etc., it appears that we can eternally preserve them. One bitter word uttered by a brother resides in our memory for days and even for years, whereas Christ's benefits and the caressing of our souls at His table are the first to be forgotten.

By means of the Lord's Supper, we are thus to progress with sanctification in general. The various and distinct branches of sanctification can be stimulated as follows:

1. If you desire to see your own weakness, insignificance, and smallness, then cast your eyes upon the Lord's Supper and meditate upon it.

a. As you partake of the Lord's Supper, presume and even judge yourself to be poor, feeble, and insignificant, and then by analogy consider how we normally conduct ourselves. If, for instance, you have a sufficient quantity of ointment in the house, would you then run to the doctor—or, by analogy, to Christ? Or why would you go to your neighbor for bread if you have always enough of a supply in your own pantry? Our form for the Lord's Supper therefore states it so well: "Considering that we seek our life out of ourselves in Jesus Christ, we acknowledge that we lie in the midst of death"; that means that we are as incapable of saving ourselves as a dead person is capable of reviving himself.

b. If by the grace of God you may already have a measure of spiritual life and faith, etc., it will yet be so weak and feeble that it must daily be sustained by such visible, tangible, and appetizing means. If someone must continually make use of crutches, may he then boast that all is well with his own legs? Is it not so that looking at his crutches will sufficiently convince him that he is paralyzed and crippled? This is also true in a spiritual sense. If at times you are overcome by proud and conceited thoughts, then suppress them by considering your need of the Lord's Supper. Think to yourself, "What measure of goodness is there in me if it needs to be maintained and sustained by a continual supply of food, lest it should decline?"

2. If you wish to be led to a livelier abhorrence of your sins, then consider

a. that the breaking of the bread and the pouring of the wine in the Lord's Supper signify the abuse, breaking, and killing of the body of our Lord Jesus Christ as well as the shedding and pouring forth of His blood. Consider that all this occurred solely because of your sin. You will then consider how abominable sin must be, for neither animals, nor people, nor children of a king, but rather God Himself, the creator of heaven and earth, the savior of the world, etc. had to suffer, be crucified, killed, and descend into hell. How very much God's nature and glory must indeed have been impugned by sin! Its measure is such that if either the entire world or all of the angels in heaven or whatever else would be of even greater value were to have intervened, made satisfaction, or were destroyed, then atonement or reconciliation could not possibly have been achieved in that way! Consider furthermore that this breaking of the bread and the outpouring of the wine at the Lord's Supper displays visibly, as in a painting, that your smallest sinful thought could not have been atoned for if all the angels of heaven would immediately have been willing to become devils and allowed themselves to be cast into the abyss of hell. Instead, it communicates that it is according to God's will that precisely that body and blood which is set before you in the Lord's Supper is ordained to be the atonement for your sin. And if this is true for the least sinful thought, we cannot begin to fathom how utterly abominable and accursed the entire mass of our sins must be.

b. also the fact that you are a personal recipient at the Lord's Supper. Not only are the bread and wine taken, broken, shed forth, and given, but with your own hands and mouth you yourself may take and receive the same. Consider then in all of this your personal involvement in the torturing, scourging, killing, and crucifixion of your savior. Not only did all of this actually occur, but you yourself have participated in it. Therefore, as truly as you receive with your own hands the elements, so you with your own hands have captured, tried, and scourged Him. You have mocked and spat upon Him. Yes, you have crucified Him, and you have, as it were, cast Christ into hell. The Jews would never have been so vicious and barbaric against Him if you had not handed Him to them to be scourged. Furthermore, an angry God would never have so manifested His wrath toward Him, nor would the devil have so raged against Him, if your own sins had not truly provoked Him to do so. All this is signified when you personally receive the tokens of the Lord's Supper and partake of them. Oh, how bitterly you then will have to weep when you truly take to heart that you yourself have pierced and murdered your God, your greatest friend, and yes, your savior, etc.! Then you will see what it means for you to sin. To sin is nothing less than to murder and kill Him, and, as much as is in you, to inflict afresh upon His soul the terrors of hell. This is as certainly true as that you partake of the Lord's Supper with your own hands.

3. If you want your faith to be more lively, then in regard to the Lord's Supper consider:

a. that God takes special care—and how tender His concern is—to provide at each celebration of the Lord's Supper such visible, clear, and stable supports and reinforcements. At times you may think that you have such a small beginning that the time will come when all will vanish, and that you will no longer be able to maintain a lively disposition, etc. However, take notice how the Lord remains involved. Though you yourself may at times forget Him, He will nevertheless not forget you. He still offers you His help in providing your faith with nourishment that is readily available. He deals with you as He did with Thomas. If you cannot believe that He is yours, He will let you see, feel, and taste that He is yours. "The bread which we break is…the communion of the body of Christ."[1] God could have considered it sufficient to give you faith. But no, He also watches over this faith, and as the faithful Father of your spiritual being He provides you with food and drink.

b. how the benefits of the Lord's Supper are appropriated to you in a personal and unique way. "Take, eat: this is my body, which is broken for you.… This cup is the new testament in my blood. Do this as often as you drink it in remembrance of me."[2] This special application, revealing that you are truly and personally also the murderer of Christ, reveals that you are indeed personally redeemed and delivered by Him, for the one is contingent upon the other. There is no one who by his sins has put Christ to death, but that this same death is not for him also the atonement for his sins. Then why do you not believe, and why do you doubt any longer? The bread and wine are given to you in particular, and so is the blood and body of Christ.

c. who it is that makes you the personal beneficiary of all this. It is Christ Himself, the searcher of the heart, the Son of God, and the mouth of truth. To receive the bread and wine from the minister is nothing less than to receive it in the name of Christ. There is therefore not the least deceit hidden in this, that is, as long as you are a true partaker of the Lord's Table. If the minister were personally to appropriate this to you, you could be mistaken; but now Christ, who cannot lie, does all this by means of the minister. How then can you be deceived? However, we already have addressed this more extensively in the preceding.

d. to what end such personal appropriation occurs in the Lord's Supper.

i. A bloody seal is thereby placed into your hand of the wondrous, eternal, and salvific covenant of grace that God has established with you in Christ. Furthermore, it seals all the

---

1. 1 Cor. 10:16.
2. 1 Cor. 11:24–25.

comforting promises that issue forth from this covenant for all God's children. For, as someone has stated, the believer may observe that it is the most earnest desire of the Lord our God to assure him of His extraordinary favor toward him. Therefore, in addition to His Word, which is sure, the Lord in His abundant mercy has also instituted holy baptism and the Lord's Supper so that the believer may indeed be greatly comforted. It therefore cannot be any different but that whenever the Christian carefully considers the occasion of baptism and the Lord's Supper, he will be increasingly assured of God's grace and favor toward him personally. This is similar to someone not merely receiving a promise but also receiving a carefully sealed letter in which many wonderful things are promised to him by a faithful and powerful person. Whenever he now looks at or thinks about this sealed letter, he will be increasingly assured that he has a claim to the matters that are being promised in the letter, namely, that these matters shall be his and that it shall not be in vain to demand them from the one who has promised them.

ii. The purpose of your partaking of the Lord's Supper is to set before your eyes the most intimate union that exists between you and the Lord Jesus Christ, a union that has been cemented by the Holy Spirit. When someone eats, not only is there a close interaction between the food that is being eaten and the one eating it, but that same food will partially be transformed into his own substance. Consider therefore what it means for you to eat the body of the Lord Jesus and to drink His blood so that you would trust all the more in Him with whom such a very intimate union has been established. There is also an intimate relationship between husband and wife. How can we actually express what that union consists of? And yet how can that compare to the union we may have with Christ when we eat His flesh and drink His blood? The husband neither eats his wife, nor the wife her husband. The body and blood of the one is not spiritual food and drink for the other, as is so in this spiritual union with Christ. Yes, however intimate spouses may be with one another, they nevertheless have each their own soul. The soul of the husband is not the soul of the wife, and the wife has a soul that is not the husband's. However, our union with Christ is quite another and a far superior matter. By eating His flesh and drinking His blood, we become of one spirit with Him (1 Cor. 6:17). His Spirit is our spirit, and our spirit is His. "For by one Spirit are we all baptized into one body."[3] How would we not believe all the more firmly in what the proper use of the Lord's Supper teaches us, namely, that He has become one with us in such a fashion as we ourselves experience it?

4. Is it your desire to be more obedient to God?

a. Consider then in the Lord's Supper who the person is with whom you are so intimately united. Consider how pure He is and not tarnished by any form of disobedience. How it behooves you therefore to resist as little as possible the will of Him with whom you are so intimately united! When you truly meditate upon this, can you then possibly love what He hates and hate what He so tenderly loves? This would truly be as if you desired to oppose yourself, since you are flesh of His flesh and bone of His bones. To be disobedient toward God, while desiring simultaneously to be the beneficiary of the perfect obedience of Christ, is nothing less than desiring to combine light and darkness, God and Satan, and virtue and sin.

b. View the broken bread and poured-out wine as signifying the broken, abused, and murdered body of Christ. Resolve then that you no longer will live in the sins that caused Him to be so cruelly abused and slain. Ask yourself, "Can I overlook those monsters, thieves, and murderers of God who are symbolized to us in such a lively manner in the Lord's Supper, where I still smell the blood of my faithful Savior? Should the great lover of men have hung on the cross as a spectacle to angels and men, have groveled in His blood, have crawled on the earth as a worm, have endured the sparks of hell flying around His ears, and endured them in His soul? Should these trouble-makers and instigators of all this evil still remain on the throne of my heart? Given that He has

---

3. 1 Cor. 12:13.

been cursed for my sins, should those who cursed Him be honored, stimulated, and caressed? Far be it from me!" You will think, "How abominable this would be!" You should counter this therefore by seeking to subdue increasingly all that which is identified by the Lord's Supper as having contributed to the murdering and bruising of your very own Lord.

c. Behold also in the entire Lord's Supper—in this plentiful meal and these heavenly pre-nuptials—the streams and brooks of God's lovingkindnesses! Then consider this: "This transaction reveals to me that God has fully given Himself to me. How then could there be anything in me that I would not wholeheartedly give to Him? If in all this He does what I desire, that is, as much as is subservient to my salvation, should I then not also do His will? If by faith I receive Him into my heart as truly as I cause the bread to enter my body by way of my mouth, should He then encounter a rebellious and disobedient heart, one that conspires against Him and is unwilling to permit Him to rule as King? No, indeed not! I would rather exclaim with David, "What shall I render unto the LORD for all his benefits toward me?" (Ps. 116:12); "I will run in the way of your commandments, for you will enlarge my heart" (Ps. 119:32).

5. If, by means of the Lord's Supper, you also desire to grow in patience, so that you will neither murmur nor grieve when God afflicts you, then compare

a. your suffering with the breaking, crucifixion, and killing of the body of Christ that you may eat in the Lord's Supper. Consider, then, how insignificant your affliction is when compared with His. Where are your scourgings? Where are your crowns of thorns? Where are your drops of blood? Where has God been opposed to you as a provoked judge? When have you experienced hell in your soul? When have you been forsaken by all your friends? Where are the stripes, wounds, etc., on your back? Where have you been seated at one table with your traitor? When have your enemies been your judges? When did you receive gall and vinegar for your refreshment? And finally, where did you die on an accursed cross? Compare your suffering once with all this, and consider whether your cross is not merely one made of straw and feathers in comparison with His iron and accursed cross? And what else would we not be able to add if we were inclined to enlarge upon this?

b. and observe also in the Lord's Supper the willingness of Christ in all His sufferings and how readily and unreservedly He surrendered Himself. He as willingly surrendered His body and blood, whereof the bread and wine are seals, as these are given to you by the minister. He was led as a lamb to the slaughter, and as a sheep before her shearers is dumb, so He opened not His mouth (Isa. 53:7). Instead, "He humbled himself, and became obedient unto death, even the death of the cross" (Phil. 2:8). "Behold," so He spoke, "I delight to do your will, O my God" (Ps. 40:8). There is no part in His suffering to which He was compelled to submit, even as the minister is not compelled to distribute the bread at the Lord's Supper. When considering this, should you then, as it were, have to be dragged by your hair in order to follow Him when often you have to endure no more than a sour face or a sharp word for the sake of His truth, or even when you have to endure a fever, an illness, or whatever else might be?

6. Is it also your desire that a greater love toward your neighbor would be stirred up within you? Then consider

a. the love of Christ toward you in the Lord's Supper, you who were indeed His creature but through sin have become His enemy and murderer. And consider that you nevertheless have not been rejected by Him, but rather, by His grace, have been called back and accepted by Him. Consider how often you are being fed and satisfied by that very body that previously, because of your sins, was so grievously murdered and mutilated! You should then think the following: "If God has loved me to such an extent, then I am obliged to love my brethren, and not only my brethren, but also my enemies. Also by way of this broken bread, Christ is set before us as having died for us when we were yet sinners. If Christ, then, has given His soul and body to me who hated Him, should I then not be willing to give to those who hate me even my money, my favor, and all other assistance?" Did not our Savior say, "Love your enemies, bless them that curse you, do good to them that hate you, and pray for them which despitefully use you, and persecute you; that you may be the children of your Father which is in heaven. For he makes his sun to rise on the evil and on the good, and sends rain on the just and on the unjust. For if you love them which love you, what reward do you have? Do not even the publicans do the same? And if you salute your brethren only, what do you do more than others? Do not even the publicans do the same? Be perfect therefore, even as your Father which is in heaven is perfect" (Matt. 5:44–48)?

b. how the Lord's Supper confirms your most intimate union with all the saints. "For we being many are one bread, and one body, for we are all partakers of that one bread" (1 Cor. 10:17). The bread used in the Lord's Supper is made up of many kernels of wheat, and yet it is but one bread, and there is one wine that is made of many berries having been pressed together. This illustrates that all true believers, though many in number, nevertheless constitute one corporal entity or body. "For no man ever hated his own flesh; but he nourishes and cherishes it, even as the Lord cherishes the church" (Eph. 5:19). From this it necessarily follows that all the good you do toward your brother is doing good toward yourself. Since the Lord's Supper displays that you are truly one, even as the many wheat kernels become one bread through the baking process and the many berries that are pressed together become one wine, the contradiction is then monstrous when all who are members of this same body are at odds with one another through hatred, envy, quarreling, fighting, etc., though the one may indeed be even more wretched and despised than the other.

Paul therefore addresses this matter in great detail, saying, "For the body is not one member, but many. If the foot shall say, Because I am not the hand, I am not of the body; is it therefore not of the body? And if the ear shall say, Because I am not the eye, I am not of the body; is it therefore not of the body? If the whole body were an eye, where were the hearing? If the whole were hearing, where were the smelling? But now has God set the members every one of them in the body, as it pleased him. And if all were one member, where were the body? But now are they many members, yet but one body. And the eye cannot say unto the hand, I have no need of you; nor again the head to the feet, I have no need of you. No, much more those members of the body, which seem to be more feeble, are necessary. And those members of the body which we think are less honorable, upon these we bestow more honor; and our unpresentable parts have more modesty. For our presentable parts have no need. But God has knitted the body together, having given more abundant honor to that part which lacked it that there should be no schism in the body, but that the members should have the same care one for another. And if one member suffers, all the members suffer with it; or if one member is honored, then all the members rejoice with it. Now you are the body of Christ, and members individually" (1 Cor. 12:14–27).

CHAPTER

6

Thus, we have set before you how, by virtue of God's gracious cooperation, the Lord's Supper in many ways is efficacious in rendering us more fruitful and holy.

I want to conclude by briefly dismantling several objections to what I have just addressed.

Objection #1: I am ignorant of how the Lord's Supper is efficacious toward sanctification. Regardless of whether I have partaken for the first or tenth time, I remain unaffected.

Answer: 1. If someone can say so casually that this is completely foreign to him, then I dare say that such a person has little reason to believe he has ever partaken of the Lord's Supper in truth. Should such a person desire to detect this in his heart, may it then please the Lord at some point to grant him a measure of such fruit.

2. If these are the words of a concerned soul, then I wish to counsel her to refresh her memory and to determine whether she may have forgotten the effect the Lord's Supper did have upon her. Such forgetfulness can frequently be caused by temptations, spiritual desertion, or other causes. It may also be that such a soul suspects what she perceives in herself, because it fell short of what she expected and thus has concluded that it was not of the right kind. Weak Christians commonly err in this regard.

3. Not everyone experiences the efficacy of the Lord's Supper in regard to both sanctification and spiritual joy in the same

measure. We already observed this in the preceding with regard to spiritual joy.

4. In regard to sanctification, one can grow either upward or downward, for "the remnant that is escaped of the house of Judah shall again take root downward and bear fruit upward" (Isa. 37:31). The first occurs when there is a greater abundance of visible fruits, such as the exercise of faith, love, etc. The other occurs when we are troubled and grieved more intensely and passionately about our spiritual deficiency than has previously been the case. It is then that the root of sanctification, a genuine and spiritual humbling of one's self, takes root downward deeper and deeper into the soil of our heart. Even when there is neither upward nor outward growth, a tree still may be truly growing. What matters is whether it then grows downward, causing its roots to be entrenched all the more thoroughly. It can possibly be that by partaking of the Lord's Supper you frequently do not grow upward, but rather that you have decreased in your own estimation and have been exercised more deeply with your deficiencies. I have stated some evidences of this earlier. Or, your complaint may possibly be that your partaking of the Lord's Supper has yielded so little progress in holiness.

5. It could also be that your sanctification is that vigorous that you may not notice that you are progressing by each successive participation in the Lord's Supper. It is always true that the weak and the young can discern their increase in strength much more readily than someone who already is strong and mature.

Additional Objection: I am, however, declining, and when I consider how it was when I began to partake of the Lord's Supper and compare it to how it is now, I can hardly conclude that there is any significant difference. What is true, however, is that I have become more lethargic, sluggish, and worldly.

Answer: 1. It is truly to be lamented if such is indeed the case, and it is high time that you "lift up the hands which hang down, and the feeble knees..." (Heb. 12:12). It can, however, also be a season similar to the one in which Christ confronts the angel of the

church of Ephesus. He first greatly praised him, saying, "I know…
your labor, and your patience…and for my name's sake [you] have
labored and have not grown weary" (Rev. 2:2–3). However, He
then rebukes him for having left his first love.

2. It may seem to you that you are regressing after the Lord's Supper,
even though in actuality this is not the case. Solomon says, "there is
one that makes himself poor, yet has great riches" (Prov. 13:7).

a. It may be that your body will be weaker and more feeble after
the Lord's Supper than beforehand, so that the spirit may be equally
willing but the flesh will be weaker. He who has to do his work with
a dull saw can be very willing to do his work, and yet be troubled
by discouragement and listlessness in doing so. This is not to be
blamed on the one who does the work, but rather on the tool which
is unsuitable for the task. Likewise, a soul can be as inclined toward
holiness and yet have more difficulty to bring this into practice than
before the Lord's Supper because the body, the soul's instrument if
you will, does not cooperate as much as she would desire.

b. You may think that your corruption is manifesting itself
more—not because this is so, but because there are increased reasons and situations that will provoke its manifestation. You may
possibly feel more bitter toward your neighbor than before, not
because there was less of that disposition of bitterness in your heart
than before, but because your neighbor may never before have
wronged you as much as now. There will then be a rush of exas-
peration and anger such as you had not encountered before, and
you possibly now have to conclude that there never had been such
an occasion for such bitterness.

c. You may consider yourself to have regressed—not because
this indeed is the case, but because someone else with whom you
were either on a par or excelled spiritually has now made such
unusual progress in grace that he has now surpassed you. In
observing this, you now judge yourself to be all the more deficient,
because someone more deficient than you now excels you. This is,
however, not necessarily the case, for you truly could be the same
and may even have improved, though another may yet excel you.
For example, you may have advanced three degrees in the faith,

and another but two. It can happen, however, that the other person advances another two degrees, so that he who earlier lagged behind is now ahead of you. You, however, did not regress, but rather maintained the status quo.

3. It can also be that you may deem yourself to have regressed spiritually after the Lord's Supper when in reality you have made progress. For

a. upon approaching God in as solemn a manner as you do in the Lord's Supper, you will have received more light and a clearer view in your soul so that you now perceive many corruptions that you were previously unable to discern. However, a clearer view of your corruptions does not mean regression but, rather, progression. If a room is very filthy and one enters it with a candle to clean it, he will see and find much more dirt than he had previously detected. However, this does not mean that the room is filthier than before, but rather that steps are now being taken to make it all the more clean.

b. upon partaking of the Lord's Supper, you may possibly have a much more tender and sensitive conscience than previously was the case. Your heart will now beat more rapidly about various sins to which you paid but little attention previously. Perhaps an angry word at present is troubling to you, whereas earlier you had little or no concern regarding cursing and slandering. Such increased tenderness and sensitivity of heart is not deterioration but, rather, advancement.

Objection #2: However, if all were well with me, I would be of a different disposition. After each Lord's Supper I would have made some progress, and how advanced in grace I then already ought to be!

Answer: 1. It is your obligation to do your part in making progress in sanctification after each Lord's Supper. If, however, contrary to your desire, there are some deficiencies in your performance of this duty, you must therefore not be too hasty in condemning your entire attendance at the Lord's Table.

2. Nowhere has God promised that He will grant a greater measure of grace at each administration of the Lord's Supper. It is indeed the objective of the Lord's Supper to nurture this. However, since the Lord's Supper is but a means of moral persuasion, it will always depend on God's sovereign disposition whether the use of this means will have the desired effect. The Lord's Supper is indeed a means of grace, and it should therefore be used as such. But it is no more than a means. It is not the primary cause of such a blessing, and one should therefore not expect to receive it solely by the use of this means.

Objection #3: Often I fall into sin more readily after the Lord's Supper than beforehand. How can I then conclude that my partaking has been efficacious unto sanctification?

Answer: You may occasionally have received more spiritual strength and yet have more readily fallen into sin. It could be

1. that as a result, you more readily trusted in yourself, and God, in order to stir up a greater measure of grace, has therefore withdrawn His influence in some measure so that your pride will be curbed.

2. that in proportion to a greater measure of spiritual strength you will also be subjected to more and stronger temptations and enticements toward sinning.

3. that after the Lord's Supper you will all too frequently find within yourself a fear for sinning which is both excessive and fueled by unbelief, causing you to stumble all the more readily. This would be analogous to someone washing stemware, for he who does this too fearfully will break it as readily as one who does this carelessly. Or, he who walks too cautiously upon ice will fall as readily as another who walks across it too confidently. He who has a most scrupulous conscience will therefore be the first one to stumble. You need to understand that I am here referring to an unbelieving timidity rather than a believing carefulness in regard to sin.

Objection #4: Sometimes I will increasingly refrain from sin shortly after my partaking of the Lord's Supper. This will decline, however, when in some measure it begins to fade from my memory. How can it then be that I have progressed in sanctification as a result of the Lord's Supper?

Answer: In no wise do I wish to excuse such serious decline. Such a decline is very common among the regenerate as well as the unregenerate; however, there is a very obvious difference.

1. This is frequently true with unregenerate participants. They know that the offense of their sins and the godly person's abhorrence of it will not be as great when considerable time has expired after the administration of the Lord's Supper, as will be the offense of their sins committed shortly thereafter. They think that their commission of sin will not cause as much harm and shame, and therefore they will sin all the more easily. However, with regenerate participants, this is often caused by a simple forgetting of the motives not to sin, motives such as should have been stimulated by their partaking of the Lord's Supper. As time transpires, their reflection upon these motives will no longer be as lively, and this will cause them to slacken a bit more.

2. The regenerate also sigh about such decline, which is rarely the case with the unregenerate. There are those who believe it to be only reasonable that one begins to relax a bit more when some time has expired after the Lord's Supper. Such consider it to be fitting that immediately following such holy activity, one would refrain from sinning to some extent. However, they consider it to be too strict and demanding that one should always be so zealous and live beyond reproach.

Objection #5: At the very best, there is with me some improvement in refraining from certain sins, but not in regard to the practice of virtue. Where is there an increase in patience, zeal, meekness, moderation, courage, carefulness, etc.? What progress have I made after so many Lord's Suppers, considering that these virtues constitute the essence of sanctification?

Answer: 1. If, after the Lord's Supper, you refrain from more sin than beforehand, and if your heart opposes sin, then, though you have denied this earlier, your partaking has yielded at least some progress in sanctification. For this, too, is a constituent element of sanctification. "You that love the Lord, hate evil" (Ps. 97:10); "I was also upright before him," David said, "and I kept myself from my iniquity" (Ps. 18:23); and "Abhor that which is evil" (Rom. 12:9).

2. As you know, it is our God's method to initiate sanctification with a hatred for sin, to be followed by an abstaining from sin. However, in the progression of sanctification, God follows the same order. Christ therefore said, "I am the true vine, and my Father is the husbandman. Every branch in me that bears no fruit he takes away, and every branch that bears fruit he prunes, that it may bring forth more fruit" (John 15:1–2). It should be noted that He will first lead us to an increased departure and cleansing from our sins, and thereafter to an increased practice of virtues. Be therefore not too hasty in your conclusions. Perhaps it pleases the Lord also to lead you from the one to the next, and He is already beginning to use the Lord's Supper to prompt you to abstain from more sins, so that thereafter you would bear more fruit. Add to this the words of the apostle: "Who [that is, Christ] gave himself for us, that he might redeem us from all iniquity and purify unto himself a peculiar people, zealous of good works" (Titus 2:14). Observe the order: first purification and then zeal for good works. Furthermore, "If a man therefore purge himself from these, he shall be a vessel unto honor, sanctified, meet for the master's use, and prepared for every good work" (2 Tim. 2:21). And finally, "He [that is, the angel of the covenant] shall sit as a refiner and purifier of silver; and he shall purify the sons of Levi, and purge them as gold and silver, that they may offer unto the LORD an offering in righteousness" (Mal. 3:3).

3. Perhaps you have harbored some sins in your soul that have negatively impacted the exercise of those virtues on which you are primarily focusing. If, however, by partaking of the Lord's Supper, you, as you have stated, begin to perceive a greater measure of strength to resist certain sins and are abstaining from them, then you are truly progressing toward the practice of these

worthy virtues. It is the efficacy of the Lord's Supper that yields an increased removal of all hindrances in that regard.

4. Perhaps you also observe that you are increasingly abstaining from certain sins and are practicing certain virtues. Or, it could be that the extent and enormity of these sins were such, or your commission of them has been that upsetting to you, that it transcended the taste and sweetness you previously experienced in the practice of these blessed virtues. This is often the experience of God's children. It grieves them, however, that their practice of virtue is often done with so little relish and delight that they sometimes do not even perceive that they are engaged as such. Or, it can be for a season that they cannot believe that their practice of virtue is adequate; this is a matter we have already addressed elsewhere. In such cases, it can hardly be any different than that the soul's response to the evil presently troubling her would be all the more unsettling to her, and that she takes note of this with a much greater measure of sensitivity. Such sensitivity will also be evident in regard to the practice of virtue, especially in light of the fact that for quite some time she engaged in this with so little delight and sweetness.

It is one thing to practice a certain virtue such as faith, love, and patience, but it is another thing to have the moral and inner reflection that we are rightly practicing a given virtue. The first can truly be the case, and yet we can fail to perceive the second for the aforesaid or other reasons.

Objection #6: I know not what it is that motivates me to be more careful after the administration of the Lord's Supper. It is not so much a greater love for my obligations, but perhaps having the impression that my neglect would be all the more serious, especially because by my partaking of the Lord's Supper I have committed myself to a godly walk. What does such improvement amount to that principally proceeds from merely such an impression?

Answer: 1. Such an impression may and must be in you, so that you will be all the more careful. Yes, it would be a deficiency in you if such an impression were not to move you at all.

2. It can be that such an impression will for a season move you more emotionally to love the duty you are obliged to fulfill. And yet, this is not the primary thing that causes you to be more careful. Your love toward your duty is an abiding disposition of your heart. It always resides with you and you are accustomed to this. This impression, however, is not of an abiding nature, but rather something that will reoccur from time to time. This simply illustrates that ordinarily new things move us more emotionally than things to which we are accustomed.

3. It is because of your love toward your obligation that this impression moves you so much emotionally. The reason for this is as follows: the fact that you take so seriously what you have promised at the Lord's Supper proceeds from the same love. If you did not take your obligations as seriously as you do, you would also not be so conscientious about the promises you have made.

4. To ascertain whether all of this is merely the result of an impression, or whether it proceeds from a love toward your obligation, consider then if, irrespective of such an impression, it is not your wholehearted wish and desire to live a more godly life and do those things toward which the Lord's Supper obligates you. If the latter is the case, it is then evident that this impression of what you have vowed not only affects you positively but that you are principally motivated toward that which is good. For it is indeed your desire to be more godly irrespective of what you have promised at the Lord's Table.

Additional Objection: Yes, this is what I have lamented at once, for as soon as this impression strengthens me in some measure, then almost immediately thereafter I slacken again.

Answer: Let that be as it may in regard to the doing of that which is good and the actual abstaining from evil. What nevertheless matters is whether your inclination remains steadfast and not whether you are always equally lively and zealous, and thus whether you sincerely remain so inclined. Also, the inclination toward that which is good and contrary to that which is evil can fluctuate when

the external cause by which the soul was stirred and stimulated
ceases to exert its influence. What remains, however, is an abiding
inclination that is fundamentally good and sincere even apart from
the influence of an external cause. Such a means may indeed be
used to stir up and stimulate this inclination, but it cannot be the
origin of this inclination itself.

EDIFYING DISCOURSES REGARDING THE PREPARATION FOR, THE PARTAKING OF, AND THE REFLECTION UPON THE SACRAMENT OF THE LORD'S SUPPER

Composed by

Wilhelmus à Brakel

Minister of the Gospel in Rotterdam

Printed with a meditation
by the same author

Preface to the Reader

Dear Reader,

I am hereby presenting to you an edifying treatise regarding the Lord's Supper, in which you will be instructed as to how you are to prepare yourself and both partake of and reflect upon the Holy Supper of the Lord.

It consists of three short and simple discourses regarding this matter composed by the honorable, godly, well-known, and renowned minister in God's church, Wilhelmus à Brakel. It has been my privilege to call him grandfather, and his memory continues to be a blessing to me. I found this booklet among the writings my deceased grandfather left to us.

Upon reading the above-mentioned discourses, it occurred to me that it might possibly be edifying for the general public if they were made available in print. I have therefore asked others to read them as well, so that I might also solicit their opinions. In response, I have been requested and urged to publish them, with the additional request to expand the author's framework in places, since there are sections that are too condensed—which is indeed the case. All of this has finally led me to the conclusion that I should proceed with the printing of this booklet. I have also been prevailed upon to expand this booklet to some extent. I have done this primarily in the third discourse, as it seemed to me that it needed to be expanded more than the others. Having said that, however, the essential framework is that of the author himself. I have preserved both his order and manner of approach.

I could have expanded the original text of the author even further and have added a variety of things. Instead, however, I have restricted myself only to those additions that I deemed essential in terms of getting this booklet ready for press. To go beyond this I deemed neither necessary nor useful, since it is but a brief treatise—and it would otherwise become the work of someone else.

This booklet is but a short and simple treatise—but I also consider it clear, edifying, and to the point. He who wishes to read a more extensive and different treatment of this subject matter can avail himself either of other edifying treatises or of larger books addressing this same subject matter.

This short and simple treatise can conveniently be used as a suitable handbook for the edification of plain Christian folk. This can particularly be useful during the time frame when the Lord's Supper is to be administered, although other similar edifying treatises have been published as well. I do not doubt but that this short and simple treatise will be read by some with delight and edification—especially by those who esteem and are fond of the deceased author. For them, the fact that this booklet has the name of this famous man stamped upon it as being the author is a sufficient recommendation. I therefore consider it unnecessary to recommend this any further.

It is my wish and hope that my additions will not have blemished this treatise, but rather will be viewed as being subservient to the appropriate affirmation, clarification, and expansion of the rather cryptic work of the author, and that they may be read with edification as well. After all, it has been my intent both in publishing this treatise, as well as by adding some (in my opinion) necessary and useful comments regarding certain matters, to do so for the benefit and edification of others. For that purpose, I have also added an edifying poem composed by the deceased author, being of the opinion that this would be a good fit for this booklet. Book dealer Paulus Topyn has, for the benefit of all, also added the transcript of a discourse held by the same author in a home in Leiden, which you will also be able to read with edification. This discourse gives a clear, plain, and poignant explanation of how it is only by the sovereign grace of God that a man can be converted and led to faith in Christ, and how the spiritual life of such a one will reveal and manifest itself. Its objective is that graceless people may be exposed and convicted, that the true recipients of grace may be comforted and stirred up, and that all may be instructed.

Should I observe that the publication of this work achieves its objective, there will be sufficient reason for me to be satisfied and to rejoice that by means of my initiative this treatise has been published to be read by a variety of people.

Reader, I wish you Godspeed. Use this booklet to the benefit and edification of your soul. It is thus my wish that God the Lord may bestow His blessing upon you.

I remain your well-wishing servant in the Lord,

Wilhelmus à Brakel van der Kluyt
Emeritus minister of the gospel
(Grandson of Wilhelmus à Brakel)

Sommelsdijk, April 26, 1751

Concerning Preparation for the Lord's Supper

―――――― ✻ ――――――

Question #1: What is a sacrament?

Answer: It is a sign and seal of God's covenant. Romans 4:11, "And he received the sign of circumcision as a seal of the righteousness of the faith."

Question #2: What is a divine covenant?

Answer: It is a binding agreement between God and man about man's salvation and the way in which this is attained.

Question #3: How many divine covenants are there?

Answer: There are two.

1. First, there is a covenant of works in which salvation is promised upon the condition of obedience. It was, prior to the fall, established with man in Adam and had as its seal the Tree of Life. This is expressed in Romans 10:5: "For Moses describes the righteousness which is of the law, that the man which does those things shall live by them." This covenant has been broken by sin (Rom. 8:3). However, for all who have not entered into the

covenant of grace, it demands that they be subjected to condemnation if they do not perfectly keep it. "For as many as are of the works of the law are under the curse: for it is written, Cursed is every one that continues not in all things which are written in the book of the law to do them" (Gal. 3:10).

2. In addition to this covenant of works, there is also the covenant of grace. Through Christ, the mediator of this covenant, it promises salvation gratuitously to all who believe in Him.

> Ho, every one that thirsts, come to the waters, and he that has no money; come buy and eat; yes come buy wine and milk without money and without price. Why do you spend money for that which is not bread and labor for that which does not satisfy? Listen diligently to me and eat that which is good, and let your soul take delight in plenty. Incline your ear and come unto me. Hear, and your soul shall live; and I will make an everlasting covenant with you, even the sure mercies of David (Isa. 55:1–3).

This covenant is unchangeable, unbreakable, and eternal. "For the mountains shall depart, and the hills be removed; but my kindness shall not depart from you, neither shall the covenant of my peace be removed, says the LORD that has mercy on you" (Isa. 54:10). The Old Testament sacraments of this covenant are circumcision and the Passover, and the New Testament sacraments are holy baptism and the Lord's Supper.

Question #4: What fruit does a sacrament of the covenant of grace yield?
Answer: It yields four things:

1. It brings the benefits of the covenant and the mediator of the covenant, Jesus Christ, to mind in a lively manner. By way of a visible sign, they are clearly displayed and presented.

2. It powerfully strengthens the faith whereby we appropriate the Lord Jesus Christ and His merited and gracious benefits, for not only is it a sign of this, but it is also a seal.

3. The use of the sacraments frequently yields a sweet foretaste of the promised benefits of the covenant. This occurs when the Lord, by His Spirit, enables a soul by faith to behold them with a lively hope.

4. From our side, there is the renewal of a heartfelt commitment to the Lord to pursue holiness, for by receiving and using the sacrament, we commit ourselves by renewal to live before the Lord as members of the covenant.

Question #5: What does preparation for the sacrament of the Lord's Supper consist of?

Answer: It consists of 1. self-examination, and 2. preparation.

Question #6: Is self-examination essential?

Answer: Yes, it is.

1. It is commanded in 1 Corinthians 11:28, "But let a man examine himself, and so let him eat of that bread and drink of that cup."

2. The Lord's Supper is not intended for all, but only for those who truly believe and are converted. It is a meal that Christ has ordained only for those who believe in Him, as stated in the form for the administration of the Lord's Supper.

3. A judgment is pronounced upon unworthy partakers of the Lord's Supper: "For he that eats and drinks unworthily eats and drinks judgment upon himself" (1 Cor. 11:29).

4. Many have a wrong view regarding themselves. They think they are converted, but are not; others think they are not converted, but they are.

5. Self-examination will produce a sense of gravity, concern, and fear when a person discovers that he is unconverted, and on the contrary, much liberty upon discerning that his hope of being converted is well founded.

Question #7: Are all men capable of examining themselves?

Answer: No, they are not.

1. Many are neither familiar with God's Word by which a person is to examine himself, nor with the mediator Christ; and they do not know what grace, faith, and conversion consist of.

2. Many are incapable of discerning what they either do or do not possess.

3. Many are too lazy and listless to make any effort to examine themselves as they ought.

Question #8: May the unconverted indeed partake of the Lord's Supper?

Answer: No, they may not. Thereby they provoke the Lord to wrath, "For he that eats and drinks unworthily eats and drinks judgment unto himself, not discerning the Lord's body. For this reason many are weak and sick among you, and many sleep" (1 Cor. 11:29–30).

Question #9: Who are the unconverted?

Answer: 1. All who are ignorant, and who even lack a historical knowledge of the doctrine of the gospel and of salvation. "But the natural man receives not the things of the Spirit of God, for they are foolishness unto him; neither can he know them, because they are spiritually discerned" (1 Cor. 2:14; Eph. 4:18; 5:8).

2. All who neither have a heartfelt concern nor grieve over their sinful hearts and deeds, and over the absence of God, Christ, the Holy Spirit, and spiritual life. Instead, in regard to these matters they are at ease and continue living without any concern, "feeding themselves without fear" (Jude 12). "Woe to them that are at ease in Zion and trust in the mountain of Samaria" (Amos 6:1).

3. All who have no heartfelt longing for the forgiveness of sins, comfort, communion with God, the fear of and love for God, power to do battle with sin, and a godly life. "Gather yourselves together, yes, gather together, O nation not desired" (Zeph. 2:1).

4. All who neither engage in the activities of faith nor yearn for the Lord Jesus as Mediator. They neither turn to Him in prayer and wait upon His grace nor receive Him by faith unto justification and sanctification. Neither do they surrender themselves to Him to be united to and have fellowship with Him, nor do they come to Him to be saved by Him out of free grace and by virtue of His merits. "He that does not believe is condemned already, because he has not believed in the name of the only begotten Son of God…. He that does not believe in the Son shall not see life, but the wrath of God abides on him" (John 3:18, 36).

5. All who sin blatantly or who habitually engage in a variety of lesser sins—whose thoughts, desires, intents, and pursuits only gravitate toward earthly things, and who have little or no interest in heavenly and spiritual matters. "For many walk, of whom I have told you often, and now tell you even weeping, that they are the enemies of the cross of Christ. Their end is destruction whose God is their belly and whose glory is in their shame, for they mind earthly things" (Phil. 3:18–19).

Question #10: Who must be deemed as having been converted?

Answer: For them the opposite of what has just been stated is true:

1. They have a true knowledge of the saving truths of the gospel—truths that must be known unto salvation. "But you have an anointing from the Holy One, and you know all things.... But the anointing which you have received of him abides in you, and you do not need any man to teach you; but as the same anointing teaches you of all things," etc. (1 John 2:20, 27).

2. They have a heartfelt sorrow and have a holy concern about their sins and the wretched spiritual condition they find themselves in by nature. "Blessed are they that mourn, for they shall be comforted" (Matt. 5:4).

3. They have a heartfelt desire and an earnest yearning for grace and salvation. They cannot rest unless they have sufficient grounds upon which they can be assured that they are partakers of this. "Blessed are they that hunger and thirst after righteousness, for they shall be filled" (Matt. 5:6).

4. By a true faith, they wholeheartedly choose and receive the Lord Jesus to be their mediator and savior. With soul and body they surrender and entrust themselves to Him to be justified and sanctified and to be saved solely out of free grace and by Him. "But as many as received him, to them he gave power to become the sons of God, even to them that believe on his name" (John 1:12).

5. They hate, flee, and seek to abstain from all sin and unrighteousness. Instead, they delight in, pursue, and endeavor to practice true holiness and godliness, engaging in a relentless battle

against indwelling sin, while persistently striving to make progress in sanctification (cf. Rom. 6:4, 6, 11, 17–18).

Question #11: May converted persons abstain from the Lord's Table?
Answer: No, for:

1. It is a negation of the loving invitation of Christ.

2. It is a deprivation of the comfort one would receive by partaking of the Lord's Supper.

3. It inhibits the growth of grace in their own personal lives, a growth that would thereby be stimulated.

4. It is a failure to confess the Lord Jesus, a confession we make when we do partake of the Lord's Supper.

5. It is a failure to engage in the communion of saints that would thereby be practiced.

Question #12: What are you to do if you do not know whether you are converted, being tossed between hope and fear? Should you then abstain?
Answer: To this we reply:

1. The essence of repentance and faith does not consist in being assured of them. Someone may have repented and be a believer, and yet not be assured that this is so.

2. You therefore need to examine yourself whether you engage in repenting and believing as described above, praying that the Lord would grant grace to engage in proper self-examination, so that you will not deceive yourself in a matter of such importance. Therefore, you are to examine yourselves whether you have a true knowledge of spiritual matters such as a godly sorrow, a holy yearning, and the extrinsic activities of faith—activities such as a warfare between the flesh and the Spirit, initiated by an internal hatred against sin, and a heartfelt love for pure holiness in order to live a life that is pleasing to the Lord.

3. If your conscience can affirm this to be so, then, hoping against hope, you are to rely upon God's Word, and you may be at liberty to come to the Lord's Table even if you are not fully assured of your spiritual state. By partaking of the elements, you will then

be assured that those promises are made to such a one as you are, and your faith will then be strengthened.

Question #13: Is preparation also necessary for those who do partake of the Lord's Supper?

Answer: Yes,

1. We do so for worldly wedding ceremonies, and therefore to a far greater extent we ought to do this for this spiritual wedding feast. "And he says unto him, Friend, how did you enter, not having a wedding garment? And he was speechless" (Matt. 22:12).

2. This has been commanded in similar situations: "Sanctify yourselves, and come with me to the sacrifice" (1 Sam. 16:5).

3. There is a reoccurring tendency toward decline, and therefore we continually need to be stirred up, especially at an occasion such as this, to engage in this divinely appointed work with an appropriate disposition.

4. Partaking of the Lord's Supper is an event of extraordinary solemnity—an event whereby we approach unto God.

Question #14: What can readily inhibit such preparation?

Answer: This can readily be inhibited by:

1. The postponement of this work, thinking that there will yet be sufficient time to do it.

2. Reluctance to engage in this work, thinking that other things need to be addressed first before doing this. Frequently nothing will then come of it.

3. Doubt whether one will attend the Lord's Table.

4. The power of indwelling corruption that at such a time appears to surface more strongly than ever, causing a person, so to speak, to be swept away by it.

5. A sense of impotence and unfitness when one begins to undertake the work of preparing oneself for the Lord's Table. Instead, darkness and unbelief increase, and temptations are more intense. This will cause a person to be discouraged.

6. By nature this is a very demanding task, and therefore there will be the tendency to refrain from engaging in this due to spiritual laziness.

Question #15: What does self-examination consist of?

Answer: In general, it consists in this: that you attempt to foster an attitude by which, in Christ, you may be pleasing to God. Specifically it is required that:

1. There be immediate and renewed repentance by turning away from your former life, and by lifting up your heart to God always to live a more godly life without having any desire to return to committing former sins. "Come, eat of my bread and drink of the wine which I have mixed. Forsake foolishness and live; and walk in the way of understanding" (Prov. 9:5–6).

2. In love you unite your heart to your neighbor and desist from all hatred and enmity toward your neighbor. You are to examine yourself carefully in this regard, rather than passing over this quickly, so that you will not be blinded by self-love or simply consider yourself as being innocent and putting the blame solely on your neighbor. You must also carefully consider whether someone else has an issue with you, and whether you have been the cause thereof. You must then seek to be reconciled with the offended party, and you must even take the initiative when you are older or of superior rank—or even if you are the least guilty party (cf. Matt. 5:23–24; Eph. 4:32).

3. You must have a high esteem for God's church, considering that Christ is her head, she is His purchased people, His eye is upon her, He keeps her, and He bestows His blessings upon her. You must therefore long to be with and among this people of the Lord and rejoice that you are a member of the church.

4. You must humble yourself before God due to your sins. You must reflect upon your previously sinful walk and focus upon your sins one by one, loathing and abhorring yourself due to your frequent and great sins. You must grieve over them, take the place of a worm, and in this frame confess your sins before the Lord so that you may be a suitable object of His free grace (cf. Isa. 57:15; 61:2–3; 66:2). However, outward tears and a hypocritical sorrow shall be of no avail.

5. You must immediately restore and renew your covenant with God by a renewed and repeated exercise of faith in the Lord Jesus, so that you heartily embrace Him and turn yourself over to Him, unto your justification and sanctification. You will thereby, in actuality and by renewal, enter into covenant with God in Christ.

> And they entered into a covenant to seek the LORD God of their fathers with all their heart and with all their soul. And whoever would not seek the LORD God of Israel was to be put to death, whether small or great, whether man or woman. And they swore unto the LORD with a loud voice and with shouting, trumpets, and cornets. And all Judah rejoiced at the oath, for they had sworn with all their heart and sought him with their whole desire. Then he was found of them, and the LORD gave them rest all around (2 Chron. 15:12–15).

6. You must quietly reflect upon Christ's work of redemption in an elect sinner and meditate attentively upon

a. Him as the fountain of redemption and salvation for believers.

b. Their eternal election by God.

c. The completion of Christ's work of redemption in history.

d. How He was promised as surety and mediator in the Old Testament.

e. How in the fullness of time by His obedience toward God, and particularly by His suffering and death, He has satisfied the claims of God's justice on behalf of the elect.

Reflect upon every detail of this work of redemption and upon His love that He has shown them. Reflect on its power. Reflect as well on God's purpose of glorifying Himself by the manifestation of His grace. Reflect upon the nature and steadfastness of the covenant of grace, as well as upon the nature and essence of the sacraments, particularly of the Lord's Supper. Consider how these matters are signified and sealed to the Lord's people in them.

7. Finally, pray fervently to God for a blessing upon the administration and use of the Lord's Supper, both for yourself and for the entire congregation.

SECOND DISCOURSE

Concerning the Celebration
of the Lord's Supper

※

Question #1: How should a desire to approach the table of the Lord specifically be kindled and stimulated?

Answer: Many and various things need to be taken into consideration in regard to this. You must, first of all, kindle and stimulate your desire for the Lord's Supper, so that by the use of this sacrament it may be both certain and guaranteed that you are truly a partaker of Christ and all the gracious benefits merited by Him.

Question #2: Is such assurance essential?

Answer: 1. Believers are commanded to strive for such assurance. "Examine yourselves as to whether you are in the faith. Prove your own selves. Know your own selves, how Jesus Christ is in you unless you are rejected" (2 Cor. 13:5). "Therefore, brethren, give diligence to make your calling and election sure" (2 Peter 1:10).

2. If you neglect pursuing assurance, you will become careless about your spiritual state and you will neglect being serious about your conversion.

3. Assurance is sweet, yields spiritual liberty, and kindles love to God and for holiness.

Question #3: Why is it that so many are lethargic and neglectful when it comes to seeking assurance?

Answer: This proceeds from:

1. Despondency. A person thinks, "Whatever is found in me is entirely deficient."

2. Slothfulness and laziness. A person makes no effort in this regard, and cannot be bothered making such an effort.

3. Ignorance as to how such assurance may be extracted from the Word of God.

4. Erroneously thinking that assurance can only be the result of an immediate pronouncement by the Holy Spirit.

5. Unbelieving and atheistic thoughts.

6. Unbelief. A person thinks that this will always be beyond reach; he has been praying for this so long already, and to no avail.

Question #4: How can you attain such assurance?

Answer: You must deduce this from the Word of God.

1. First, you must look for promises in the Word of God that are addressed to people who have the disposition of being poor in spirit, mourning, hungering and thirsting after righteousness, and a looking unto and believing in Jesus. You must then say, "This is true; it cannot be otherwise."

2. You must then proceed to examine your heart in the presence of God as to whether such characteristics are found in you.

3. If your conscience affirms this, then you must finally conclude from these two truths and reason as follows: "The Scriptures say that whoever is of such a disposition are those to whom such promises are addressed. Since, however, I am so disposed, this promise also pertains to me."

Question #5: What is the essence of assurance?

Answer: It consists neither in tender emotions nor in extraordinary influences of the Holy Spirit. A person may have a yearning for them, but this does not constitute the essence of assurance. Rather, it consists in:

1. A quiet peace and spiritual satisfaction resulting from the aforementioned conclusion and in having a clear grasp of the promised heavenly benefits.

2. In entrusting one's soul and salvation to Jesus, doing so without fear, and brushing aside all that may militate against this.

Question #6: What additional means are available whereby a person can, may, and must arouse and stimulate his desire and longing for the Lord's Supper?

Answer: Second,[1] you are to use such means so that, by way of the visible signs of the Lord's Supper, you may behold with your physical eye the suffering of Christ. This means beholding the necessity of this suffering, its efficacy for all the elect, and His love for them. Do this so that, by partaking of the Lord's Supper, you make a public confession before the entire world to the glory of the Lord Jesus.

Third, do this so that in love and with joy and for your personal edification you may enjoy present fellowship with Christ in the Lord's Supper, for this is the means whereby spiritual fellowship between Christ and believers is experienced. "The cup of blessing which we bless, is it not the communion of the blood of Christ? The bread which we break, is it not the communion of the body of Christ?" (1 Cor. 10:16).

Fourth, do this so that by partaking of the Lord's Supper you may have fellowship with all believers who are present and belong to other Reformed churches, irrespective of whether you know them. This occurs at the administering and partaking of the Lord's Supper: "For we being many are one bread and one body, for we are all partakers of that one bread" (1 Cor. 10:17).

Fifth, do this so that by partaking of the Lord's Supper you may increase in sanctification, for which this is a suitable and efficacious means. This comes about by the sealing of those promises of the covenant of grace that are given (that is, sealed) to us in the Lord's Supper. Among them is also this great promise: "A new heart also will I give you, and a new spirit will I put within

---

1. Relative to the first point made in question #1 of this chapter (translator).

you; and I will take away the stony heart out of your flesh, and I will give you an heart of flesh. And I will put my spirit within you, and cause you to walk in my statutes, and you shall keep my judgments, and do them" (Ezek. 36:26–27). This progression in sanctification will come about by virtue of our union with Christ as it functions in the Lord's Supper, and by your reciprocal and renewed commitment to the Lord and His service in partaking of the Lord's Supper.

Sixth, do this in response to the gracious invitation extended by the Lord Jesus to come to Him and sup with Him, when He says to us, "Come, eat of my bread and drink of the wine which I have mingled" (Prov. 9:5); "Eat, O friends; drink, yes, drink deeply, O beloved" (Song 5:1; see also Isa. 55:1–2, Matt. 11:28, Rev. 3:20).

Seventh, do this for the following reasons:

1. God the Father, by way of the Lord's Supper, comes to His children in an extraordinary manner in order graciously to reveal Himself to them.
2. The Lord Jesus comes to them in a most gracious manner to minister to them at His table.
3. The Holy Spirit is present with all His blessings.
4. The holy angels are present and delight themselves in what God is doing in the presence of His people and children.
5. The people of God are gathered in sweet fellowship, so that the location where the Lord's Supper is administered becomes nothing less than the house of God and the gate of heaven (Gen. 28:16–17).

Eighth, and finally, we are to do this because we have learned by experience that at the table it has gone well for us in the past, and we have enjoyed something that we would like to experience again.

Question #7: What are we to do when our soul is in serious disarray? When the truth has no effect upon our soul? When sin abounds and we are not affected by it with heartfelt sorrow? When we do not long for the Lord's Supper? When we are fearful of eating and drinking judgment to ourselves? When unbelieving and atheistic thoughts arise in our soul?

Answer: We are then to bare our heart before the Lord, declaring to Him how wretched our condition is, and in so doing, seek to come before Him as utterly needy and destitute. Nevertheless, we are to conduct ourselves wisely, seek to encourage ourselves, and trust in and rely upon the Word of God. We should not wander away from the Lord, for that which we desire and seek is to be found nowhere else but with Him. Instead, we are to come to the Lord's Table prayerfully and expectantly in order to see whether it would please Him graciously to meet us there and to bestow a blessing upon us.

Question #8: How are we to approach the Lord's Table, and how are we to conduct ourselves when we partake of the Lord's Supper?

Answer: We are to do so as follows:

1. *Upon entering the church*, we must do the following:
   a. lay aside all earthly concerns and desires, and with our heart leave everything behind, also ourselves, as Abraham left Ur and Israel left Egypt; and
   b. enter as one who is approaching God Himself and entering the porch of heaven itself.

2. *Upon arising to go to the Lord's Table,*[2] we must
   a. arise as being called by the Lord Jesus, and come to Him who is calling out, "Rise up, my love, my fair one, and come away" (Song 2:10);
   b. desire to be with Jesus; and
   c. come as a bride who arises to be married to her bridegroom.

3. *Upon walking to the table*, we must
   a. reflect upon Jesus in the pathway of His suffering whereby He has merited our access to God;
   b. pray to God, saying, "Your spirit is good; lead me into the land of uprightness" (Ps. 143:10), leaning and relying upon Jesus and His promises.

---

2. The custom in Dutch churches was for those partaking of the Lord's Supper to "arise" from their pews, walk to the front of the church, and be seated at tables located there, where the elements were distributed.

4. Upon taking our seat at the table, we must view ourselves as being seated in the brightness of an open heaven from which light descends upon us at the Lord's Table, and thus as being in the presence of God and Christ. We must therefore sink away in our own insignificance and sinfulness, and be affected with filial fear and holy reverence for the Lord when considering His awe-inspiring majesty. At the same time, however, we must also cling to the covenant of grace. We are to do all of this so that we may be there to the glory of God's magnificent grace.

5. Upon eating and drinking, we must

    a. not rely upon having prepared ourselves well, but rather think little of ourselves, and derive our liberty only from the sacrifice of Christ, through whom we have secured free access to God. "In whom we have boldness and access with confidence by the faith of him" (Eph. 3:12; Heb. 4:14, 16; 10:19–22).

    b. do this as being invited by Christ to partake, saying to us, "Eat, O friends; drink, yes, drink abundantly, O beloved" (Song 5:1).

    c. not remain focused merely upon the external signs of the Lord's Supper, and yet at the same time not desist from reflecting upon them, but at once exercise faith in Christ just as we customarily do at home. This means, however, that we must then be engaged in connecting the signs to the matter that is being signified, viewing them as pledges and seals of the grace Christ has merited for us.

    d. neither expect something extraordinary nor any special movement or stirring of the Holy Spirit that would yield a great measure of light and ecstatic joy. If the Lord is pleased to grant this, it would indeed be delightful, but if not, we must be satisfied to appropriate the matters being signified by an active faith.

    e. not be too dismayed or filled with fear and trembling if there is either such an extraordinary manifestation, a concern that it will not go well with us, or anxious thoughts that suddenly overtake us. Rather, we must then set aside all misguided fear, resist the anxious thoughts that overtake us, and focus solely on reflecting upon those things that can give us courage, being conscious of the uprightness of our heart, intentions, and desires. We must believe in the steadfastness of God's covenant with us, and in so doing seek to be quiet and circumspect, waiting upon the fulfillment of God's promises.

f. Finally, upon eating and drinking, we are to make a conscious and believing use of Jesus Himself, embracing Him by faith and thereby uniting ourselves to Him. We are to do so by magnifying God's free grace, the efficacy of Christ's atonement, the steadfastness of the covenant of grace, and the reliability of the sign that is being given to us as a seal. We are then to say, "This is indeed true, and Jesus is sealing this to me at this very moment."

6. *Upon arising from the table and departing*, we must

a. say in our heart, "My Jesus shall keep His Word. I am satisfied with this and rely upon it. 'You will guide me with your counsel, and afterward receive me to glory'" (Ps. 73:24).

b. have a desire always to remain in the presence of the Lord Jesus and to leave our heart with Him.

c. comfort ourselves with His return in judgment, when He will forever take us to Himself in glory.

d. depart as one having been sent by the Lord Jesus to proclaim His glory among the people, to testify of His virtues, and thus to be engaged before the entire world in doing His work and reflecting His image in our lives.

Concerning Reflection
upon the Lord's Supper

―――――――――― ⚜ ――――――――――

Question #1: Is it necessary to reflect upon the Lord's Supper?

Answer: Yes, we must, for:

1. God's Word commands us to meditate and reflect upon those benefits we have received from Him. Moses earnestly exhorted Israel to do so: "And you shall remember that the LORD your God led you all the way these forty years in the wilderness.... When you have eaten and are full, then you shall bless the LORD your God for the good land which he hath given...you. Beware that you forget not the LORD your God" (Deut. 8:2–11). David exhorted himself in this regard: "Bless the LORD, O my soul, and forget not all his benefits" (Ps. 103:2).

2. When we meditate and reflect upon the Lord's benefits, it will make us grateful so that we must say with the psalmist, "What shall I render unto the LORD for all his benefits toward me...? I will offer to you the sacrifice of thanksgiving" (Ps. 116:12, 17).

3. Meditating upon God's benefits will yield much liberty to approach God, asking and beseeching Him to bestow more of His benefits upon us. It will also stimulate us to do our work with the confidence that the Lord will give His help and assistance in the

future, considering the benefits He has previously bestowed upon us. Such was David's experience (1 Sam. 17:37).

4. It will stimulate and motivate us to pursue holiness and a godly walk before the countenance of the Lord. Indeed, when we consider the Lord's benefits that have been bestowed upon us, they obligate us to serve and obey Him most willingly as our benefactor. The psalmist expresses this when he says, "For you have delivered my soul from death, mine eyes from tears, and my feet from falling. I will walk before the LORD in the land of the living" (Ps. 116:8–9).

Question #2: Wherein does reflection upon the Lord's Supper consist?

Answer: This consists in the performance of various duties to which we are obliged after having partaken of the Lord's Supper; that is, to behave ourselves well accordingly.

Question #3: What are the special duties that constitute reflection upon the Lord's Supper?

Answer: Specifically, reflection consists in 1) meditating and remembering; 2) gratitude toward God; 3) being near to God and having fellowship with Him; 4) despising and forsaking the world; and 5) displaying by our conduct that we are Christians, and as such are in covenant with the Lord.

Question #4: What should be our first activity after having partaken of the Lord's Supper?

Answer: There should be a quiet and calm reflection upon and remembrance of those things upon which we ought to be meditating.

Question #5: What are the things that we should be reflecting upon and remembering?

Answer: We should first of all attentively and calmly reflect upon the steadfastness and immutability of the covenant of grace, and upon all its promises that have been sealed to us by means of the Lord's Supper, such as the forgiveness of sins, comfort, sanctification, and the guidance of the Holy Spirit. Additional promises pertain to God's preservation of believers in the state of grace, as well as to the eternal salvation in heaven that shall be their portion after this life.

Question #6: To what must the reflection upon these matters be subservient, and what must its ultimate objective be?

Answer: We are to reflect calmly and believingly upon these things, so that this will stimulate us to rely confidently upon the faithfulness of God and Christ in regard to the keeping of their promises, expecting their fulfillment believingly, with a lively hope, and with patience.

Furthermore, it should stimulate us to be faithful in the keeping of our promises made to the Lord during and by way of our partaking of the Lord's Supper, namely, that being in covenant with Him, we wish to walk before Him in true holiness, so that with good courage and joy we may run the race that is set before us in order thereby to secure and enjoy the eternal glory of heaven, knowing that our labor is not in vain in the Lord (1 Cor. 15:58).

Question #7: What else ought we to reflect upon?

Answer: Second,[1] we must reflect upon and remember what our spiritual frame was during our preparation for and during the actual celebration of the Lord's Supper. We are to consider whether we were earnest and diligent or feeble and barren, whether we were sorrowful and tender or hard and insensitive, whether we were yearning for grace or listless and without any strong spiritual desires. What struggles between faith and unbelief did we encounter within us? What was our spiritual frame when praying to God? Was there a heartfelt resolution to repent of this or that specific sin, or were we discouraged and neither serious nor having any desires regarding this? Such are the various matters we ought to be thinking about. As a result, we will either humble ourselves before the Lord due to our deficiency, or our faith will have

---

1. The first matter to be reflected upon is found in the answer to question #5 (translator).

been strengthened and we will have been stimulated to express our gratitude toward God—both in proportion to what we have discovered while reflecting.

Question #8: Is there anything else that ought be the object of our reflection?

Answer: Third, we should meditate upon and remember what the Lord's dealings with our soul either have or have not been at that moment. Did we receive peace and quietness in our soul, or was there inner agitation? Did we experience peace with God in our heart, or did the Lord hide Himself from us? Did He bestow upon us the enjoyment of being assured of our fellowship with Him, or did He permit our soul to be in a doubtful frame? Did He grant joy in our heart, or was our soul filled with sorrow, causing us to cry out unto the Lord? Did we receive much light from the Lord, or did our soul dwell in darkness? Was our heart tender toward spiritual matters, or were we only able to exercise our faith regarding this or however else it may have been with us? This will prompt us to inquire why we did not enjoy much spiritual refreshment, and there will be an acknowledgement of the Lord's sovereignty in bestowing His grace upon us, as well as gratitude for the blessings we received to a greater or lesser degree.

Question #9: What also belongs to a reflection upon the Lord's Supper?

Answer: Gratitude to God for all the goodness He has manifested toward us.

Question #10: In what does such gratitude consist?

Answer: This consists in:

1. A thoughtful reflection upon and consideration of all the benefits we have received, as well as their goodness and magnitude, esteeming them highly: "I will remember your wonders of old. I will also meditate on all your work and talk of your doings" (Ps. 77:11–12; also see Pss. 139:17; 143:5).

2. Recognizing the possession of the blessings we have received, so that we may retain our assurance that we truly have become

partakers of both the great benefit of having been reconciled through Christ, as well as the benefits of the covenant of grace, and that we experienced a good spiritual disposition toward and fellowship with God (Gal. 2:20).

3. Recognizing that God has been the giver of these blessings, as well as recognizing His sovereignty in bestowing them upon us, a people as unworthy as we are. All of this will fill us with holy amazement (see Gen. 32:10; 2 Sam. 7:18; 1 Chron. 29:13–14).

4. Spiritual and holy joy before God in regard to what we have received and enjoyed, irrespective of its degree (see Isa. 61:10; 1 Sam. 2:1; Luke 1:46–49).

5. An inclination to reciprocate, giving ourselves as a sacrifice unto the Lord and His service (see Ps. 116:12–13, 16; Rom. 12:1).

6. Praising and magnifying the Lord for His goodness and sovereign grace (see Pss. 103:1–2; 145:4; Eph. 1:3).

7. Speaking to others at appropriate occasions of the goodness the Lord has bestowed upon us (see Pss. 66:16; 145:4–7; Isa. 12:4).

Question #11: What else belongs to this work of reflection?

Answer: To this also belongs a continual and holy walk and fellowship with God.

Question #12: What does such walking and having fellowship with God consist in?

Answer: It consists in:

1. Being neither able nor willing to find any true enjoyment other than in God, and that we consider, seek, and find our chief delight and pleasure only in being in His blessed nearness in fellowship with Christ, so that we truly may testify before the Lord with Asaph, "Whom have I in heaven but you? And there is none upon earth that I desire beside you. My flesh and my heart fail, but God is the strength of my heart and my portion forever.... But it is good for me to draw near to God" (Ps. 73:25–26).

2. Having a continual and lively impression that God in Christ has become our God, so that with David we can and must say before the Lord, "O God, you are my God" (Ps. 63:1).

3. A continual turning to the Lord regardless of where we are or what we are doing, always being desirous that our heart and mind are focused on Him and longing and anticipating how in grace He will be pleased to reveal Himself to us. This was true for David, who said, "Mine eyes are ever toward the LORD" (Ps. 25:15), and for the church: "Therefore I will look unto the LORD; I will wait for the God of my salvation" (Mic. 7:7).

4. Continually having a lively impression of God in our heart, attentively focusing upon and considering His majesty, holiness, righteousness, omniscience, omnipotence, wisdom, goodness, and other of His attributes and perfections. He is therefore worthy of being honored by us and all creatures. David testifies of this (or the Messiah testifies regarding Himself) in Psalm 16:8: "I have set the LORD always before me."

5. Always conducting ourselves before the Lord our God as we ought, so that we will consistently have the highest esteem for Him, love Him with all our heart as our God and our highest good, fear Him with a filial fear, and always have a deep sense of awe and a holy reverence for Him in our hearts. All of this will manifest itself in our conduct. We will wholeheartedly endeavor to obey and be subject to Him in all we are called either to do or not to do. We must therefore be quiet, submissive, and patient under all His dealings with us, so that in so doing we may honor, serve, and glorify Him as we ought and thus may live in a manner that is pleasing to Him. We are to do as God commanded Abraham to do: "I am the Almighty God; walk before me and be perfect" (Gen. 17:1), and as David declared that he would do: "I will walk before the LORD in the land of the living" (Ps. 116:9).

6. Continually engaging in a holy and spiritual fellowship with Him by repeatedly taking the liberty to come to Him, repeatedly pursuing a spiritual dialogue with Him, making all our needs and holy desires known to Him, praying and beseeching Him for all that we need and desire, and seeking His counsel in all unsettling

situations and waiting upon His answers. We will feel ourselves in all things dependent upon Him and will delight ourselves in Him by engaging in such interaction with the Lord. This is acquainting ourselves with the Lord as Eliphaz urged Job to do: "Acquaint now yourself with him, and be at peace; thereby good shall come unto you" (Job 22:21).

7. Finally, it consists in finding in God our highest good and all-sufficient portion, in enjoying His blessed fellowship and nearness, in doing so with complete pleasure and without either desiring or seeking anything outside of Him as our highest good. In all cases, we will then also place our highest trust in Him alone, quietly and without fear submitting to and trusting in His leading as David did: "Truly my soul waits upon God; from him comes my salvation. He only is my rock and my salvation; he is my defense; I shall not be greatly moved.... In God is my salvation and my glory; the rock of my strength and my refuge is in God" (Ps. 62:1–2, 7).[2] The church did likewise: "The LORD is my portion, says my soul; therefore will I hope in him" (Lam. 3:24).

Question #13: Is there something else that belongs to reflection?

Answer: Yes, it is to despise and forsake the world.

Question #14: Why are we obligated to despise and forsake the world?

Answer: We are to do so for many reasons:

1. We obligated ourselves to this when we entered into the covenant of grace. This commitment can no longer be annulled, and neither may we nor can we do so.

2. To conform to the world is spiritual adultery, and the bridegroom Jesus responds to this with holy jealousy.

3. Fellowship with the world and God cannot coexist. We must choose, forsake, or do without one of the two.

4. Cleaving to the world has already caused us so much grief that we will no longer desire to do so.

---

2. Following the numbering in the Dutch version, à Brakel gave the reference as Ps. 62:2–3, 8.

5. Cleaving to the world will bring dishonor upon the Lord our God and our Lord Jesus Christ, for thereby we act as if He were not all-sufficient for us.

6. To be detached from the world yields a special measure of freedom and happiness.

7. In so doing, we will escape many temptations at once, temptations to which we would otherwise be vulnerable.

8. When it is done out of love for Him, the Lord will richly reward such forsaking of things toward which our nature is inclined—if not in this life, then in the life hereafter.

Question #15: What does despising and forsaking the world consist in?

Answer: It consists in this: that we will consider the things of this world (that is, earthly and physical things) to be of little value. In and of themselves they are nothing but vanity. They cannot give us any genuine and complete satisfaction. Compared with heavenly and spiritual benefits, they are of no value at all. We must therefore withdraw our heart and affections from them and not be too intent on and attracted to the possession and enjoyment of them. Instead, we should be equally satisfied either without possessing them or with enjoying them. We should be willing to part with the goods of this world acquired by us when it pleases the Lord in one way or the other to take them from us, or to relinquish them when circumstances compel us to do so. The apostle John exhorts us to do this: "Love not the world, neither the things that are in the world" (1 John 2:15), and Paul tells us in Hebrews 11:24–27 that in such a fashion Moses despised and forsook the world.

Question #16: Is there not more that belongs to this?

Answer: Yes, a despising and forsaking of the world also consists in hating, abhorring, fleeing, and avoiding the immorality and vain customs of the world, as well as the sins and wicked actions committed by worldly people. This means not following suit, but rather abstaining from such irregular conduct. The apostle Paul exhorts us to do so: "Be not conformed to this world" (Rom. 12:2), and "be not therefore partakers with them…and have no fellowship with the unfruitful works of darkness, but rather reprove them" (Eph. 5:7, 11). For indeed, the grace of God teaches us to deny ungodliness and worldly lusts (Titus 2:11–12).

Question #17: Is this everything that relates to a despising and forsaking of the world?

Answer: No, for the despising and forsaking of the world consists furthermore in also hating and abhorring worldly, ungodly, unconverted, and graceless persons. This means not hating them as human beings, but as the ungodly for their ungodliness sake. David did so: "Do not I hate them, O LORD, that hate you? and am not I grieved with those that rise up against you? I hate them with perfect hatred; I count them my enemies" (Ps. 139:21–22). Therefore, we must not have a comfortable relationship with ungodly and worldly people, except when absolutely necessary. We are, however, to avoid and desist from such interaction as much as we are able, so that we will not be polluted and led astray by their company. We should primarily or exclusively keep company with the godly, thereby following David's example: "I have not sat with vain persons, neither will I go in with dissemblers. I have hated the congregation of evil doers and will not sit with the wicked" (Ps. 26:4–5); "I am a companion of all them that fear you and of them that keep your precepts" (Ps. 119:63). The Lord therefore exhorts His people, saying, "Therefore come out from among them, and be separate" (2 Cor. 6:17).

Question #18: What enables the godly to despise and forsake the world in such a fashion, a world which by nature they love as much as other people?

Answer: This comes about by means of their faith, even as Paul testifies of Moses that he did so by faith (Heb. 11:24–27). The apostle John also clearly teaches this when he writes, "For whatsoever is born of God overcomes the world; and this is the victory that overcomes the world, even our faith" (1 John 5:4). In the first place, they embrace the Lord Jesus Christ and God in Christ as their all-sufficient portion and highest good, thereby forsaking everything outside of Him. Therefore, they no longer cleave so much to the world, but rather, their heart has been loosened from it. In the second place, they behold the glory and loveliness of all spiritual benefits, and in so doing, they see how insignificant everything of this world is. In the third place, by faith they assure themselves that they are partakers of the benefits God has promised to His people, and they are confident that after this life they will arrive at the full possession and enjoyment of them. In order that they may have a better portion, they are therefore enabled, by faith, readily to forsake, despise, and abandon the world and all that pertains to it for a better portion.

Question #19: Is there anything else that belongs to reflection upon the Lord's Supper?

Answer: Yes, we must affirm publicly in all of our conduct that we are Christians and in covenant with the Lord.

Question #20: When are we called upon to make ourselves visible to the world, and in so doing demonstrate the power and fruit issuing forth from having partaken of the Lord's Supper?

Answer: We must strive to show this by our conduct in the following manner:

1. As is becoming to one who is in covenant with the Lord, we must strive to live a life of genuine holiness and godliness before the Lord our God, to be earnest and zealous in exercising all manner of Christian virtues, and with great care seek to refrain from all sins and be most earnest in battling against them. We are to do this with wisdom, prudence, in all truthfulness, with uprightness, and without self-promotion and affectation, so that by such a godly walk we may shine as lights in this world and live this life to the honor of the Lord our God. We are admonished and exhorted in all of Holy Scripture to conduct ourselves as such, even as Peter writes: "But as he who has called you is holy, so be holy in all manner of conversation; because it is written, Be holy, for I am holy" (1 Peter 1:15–16).

2. We must strive to emulate the example of Christ, for this is the obligation of a Christian who bears His Name, as is expressed in 1 John 2:6: "He that says he abides in him ought himself also so to walk, even as he walked." We must therefore strive, in the way of self-denial, to be conformed to the Lord Jesus Christ in manifesting a fervent love for God, for the godly, and for all men. We are to manifest humility in our manner of speech, in our dress, in the manner in which we order our affairs, and in whatever else there may be in which we are to be of a humble disposition. We are to manifest meekness, to be as meek as possible in our dealing with others, and therefore we must be slow to anger. We are to manifest patience and tolerance when we are mistreated rather than a vengeful spirit. We are to treat everyone in a friendly manner. We are to be peace-loving and careful to avoid all discord and disharmony. We are to show compassion toward the destitute and to be generous toward the poor and needy. We are to show benevolence toward everyone, as well as a willingness to help in whatever ways we can. The Lord Jesus practiced all these virtues and eminently excelled in them, thereby, in the words of the apostle Peter, "leaving us an example, that you should follow his steps" (1 Peter 2:21).

3. At all occasions we must publicly confess the Lord Jesus, so that rather than being ashamed of Him, we would openly and boldly, albeit prudently, take a stand for Him and His cause. We are to demonstrate that we acknowledge Him, and Him alone, to be our Lord and Savior and that we wish to be identified with Him, His church, His children, His doctrine, and His entire cause. We are to do so in spite of the fact that as a result of confessing the Lord Jesus we may, yes must, be hated, despised, and persecuted, even if we must therefore die as a martyr. We must be willing to do this so that by making such a public and bold confession of Christ we may show forth the Lord's death, thereby making Him and His glory known among men as the only and complete mediator and Savior. We must do so to His glory, to the conversion of the unconverted, and the awakening of the converted. Such is, among other things, also the duty of a Christian and partaker of the Lord's Supper, for such observation is not only his utmost obligation and of great

benefit, but it is also an utmost necessity. Every Christian therefore ought to pursue these things with diligence, being mindful of the words of the Lord Jesus: "Whosoever therefore shall confess me before men, him will I confess also before my Father which is in heaven. But whosoever shall deny me before men, him will I also deny before my Father which is in heaven" (Matt. 10:32–33).

How blessed are they who during their preparation for, their partaking of, and their reflection upon the Lord's Supper strive to conduct themselves according to what we have taught above! Every Christian and partaker of the Lord's Supper, recognizing his own impotence and unfitness, ought to be thus engaged as well as to prayerfully call upon God the Lord for the grace needed to engage in this great work. May the Lord bestow His blessing upon each one of us and grant that the reading of the preceding discourses regarding this subject matter may be subservient to what has been brought forth. Amen.

Meditation

Held on August 2, 1702, in Leiden
by Wilhelmus à Brakel

Herein is set forth how by free grace alone a man can be converted to God and be led to faith in Christ, and also how spiritual life will manifest itself in such a person.

Friends, we wish to speak a few words at this occasion. I will not preach a sermon, but I do wish to speak briefly to you about many matters. The one is an argument for and a transition to the other.

Therefore, let us begin with God's eternal purpose. The conversion of a person and the illumination of his soul by way of the gospel do not proceed from good qualifications within himself. Rather, they proceed from God's eternal good pleasure. You probably also could have said this, since you all grasp this intellectually. However, have you already learned it experientially, knowing that you neither can begin nor have begun without the Lord and that everything is granted to the elect according to God's eternal good pleasure? When someone comes under conviction and is led to God, it proceeds from this: "Yes, I have loved you with an everlasting love.

Therefore with lovingkindness have I drawn you" (Jer. 31:3). And thus, the bestowal of a greater measure of grace on this one rather than that one proceeds from eternal love, resulting in the conversion of the one and not the other.

I will focus on four words that are expressive of four activities: The *calling*, from which proceeds *regeneration*, which in turn yields *conversion*, that culminates in *holiness*. And though the Scriptures do not always make such a sharp distinction, it is yet profitable for your spiritual state to grasp the orderliness of all these matters.

Let us therefore first consider *calling*. What does it mean to call someone? Imagine a person, for example, who is traveling toward a given destination, and you know that he will be overtaken by murderers. You will call and warn him, pointing him to an alternative route where he will be safe. But what does God's calling consist of? That is nothing less than the proclamation of the gospel. This is the declaration that man, having fallen away from God, can only be delivered from eternal perdition by way of a surety. And it is the gospel that reveals the Son of God is such a surety. As surety, He has taken upon Himself human nature as well as the sins of all His elect. He has endured the punishment of which they were worthy. It is He who exclaims, "If any man thirst, let him come unto me"; "Look unto me, and be saved, all the ends of the earth"; "Come, for all things are now ready"; "For why, (O poor man) will you die?"[1] "Is this the way in which you are determined to go to hell and eternal perdition, investing your time in and attaching your heart to vain and worldly things?"

This is what constitutes the calling.

The question, however, is whether either God or Christ is calling you specifically, calling you, so to speak, by your first and last name. Perhaps there are those who think, "If only I knew that Jesus wants to receive me and that He would say to me, 'I will do everything for you that needs to be done, and I will save you.'" Then everyone being convinced of this, so you think, would hasten to take hold of Him.

---

1. John 7:37; Isa. 45:22; Luke 14:17; and Ezek. 33:11.

But my children, I wish to declare to you that Jesus is calling all who are here present, as well as all who throughout the entire world live under the ministry of the gospel. Faith is not a work within us on the basis of which God the Lord would grant us Christ, as if we would thereby be persuaded to receive Him. Children, this is not how it is. It is similar to a young man who asks a young woman to marry him. What else must such a young woman do but respond affirmatively to his proposal? This is the only thing required of her. Consider therefore that the Lord Jesus by means of the gospel is knocking and inviting you so that He may gain entrance. Therefore, if Jesus knocks and says, "Open to me," would you then not consider that person who would have Jesus knock without opening to Him to be an ungodly person?

If, therefore, we hear the inviting voice of the gospel, then all that is required is that we respond affirmatively, just as the young woman would respond to her suitor.

Friends, this evening you will be called upon to say "yes." You may possibly think, "But how do I go about this? Is it this easy to get to heaven, that is, simply by responding affirmatively to the offer of the gospel?" Yes, indeed, my friends, that is all that is needed, provided, however, that this would occur in the right way. All the unregenerate will say that they indeed want to go to heaven. However, you must know what it is to which you are to respond affirmatively. Even if this room were filled with unconverted people, they would all say, "We do indeed desire to have Jesus as our portion, for who would not desire Him?"

However, you ought quietly and calmly to consider the cost; that is, you are to consider the reasons for receiving Jesus by faith. I am still dealing with the calling, seeking to persuade you that Jesus calls each of you individually. Consider me therefore to be His servant and not as someone who merely expounds the truth for you. Consider me to be as one who speaks on His behalf, so that it is as if He Himself were present here, saying to you, "People, are you willing to believe my Word? Do you not hear my Word when I am calling out to you, 'Ho, every one that thirsteth, come to the waters; come unto me, all you that labor and are heavy laden'?"[2]

Are you not hearing this? Do not say, "I am lost, and Jesus is not calling me," for you are hearing the voice of the gospel going forth to everyone indiscriminately.

However, are there not people being called who nevertheless perish? Yes, indeed, for many are called but few are chosen. I already intended to ask you, children, whether to perish will not be a greater judgment for those who have lived under the offer of the gospel than for the Gentiles who have never heard of Christ. Concurring with the Bible, you will respond, "yes," for it shall be more tolerable for Tyre and Sidon in the Day of Judgment than for those cities in which Jesus demonstrated His power. You have answered correctly. This therefore provides me with a clear proof and argument that Jesus calls all men who live under the gospel—unless you are of the opinion that you can come in your own strength, thereby showing yourself to be of Arminian persuasion in this regard. Again, are there not people who have rejected Christ as He is offered in the gospel? (cf. Acts 13:46). How would they have been capable of rejecting Him if He had not been presented and offered to them? Does not the Savior say in John 15:22, "If I had not come and spoken unto them, they had not had sin: but now they have no cloak for their sin"?

Friends, remain focused upon your own heart. These arguments ought to persuade you fully that the Lord Jesus calls you and me and that He offers His blood and Spirit unto our salvation. Therefore, a historical faith whereby you believe that Jesus also calls you must be alive within you, even at this very moment.

But how do people respond to this calling? Many do not respond well at all. They fail to recognize that under the ministry of the Word there is a voice that calls them. The unconverted attend church; they hear the Word and read it as well. They do it as a custom, but are oblivious to the fact that God calls them in His Word, which is the reason why it bears so little fruit in their lives. Even if the least of all ministers were to expound a Bible text, even if he

---

2. Isa. 55:1 and Matt. 11:28.

were to be an unconverted man, he would nevertheless be commissioned to preach to you and set before you spiritual nourishment. Whether his offer to you is of better or lesser quality, to be called is to be called. Behold, such are they who do not acknowledge that they are being called by the Word.

There are, however, some who respond in some measure while under the Word. Their hearts become agitated to such an extent that they do not know what to make of it. They become concerned, and this concern only increases. They begin to realize that they are still unconverted, subject to God's wrath and curse, and that they are on the way to perdition. And this causes them to be perplexed. They would desire to know and ask what they must do and where they shall find Jesus.

As we said earlier, this is followed by *regeneration*. However, regeneration does not take place suddenly and instantaneously.[3]

The regeneration of a man is analogous to the original creation. We read that "the Spirit of God moved upon the face of the waters."[4] A Hebrew word is used here that refers to a hen sitting upon her eggs and in so doing bringing forth her chicks. In like fashion, the Spirit of God gradually brought forth all creatures.

This also is how regeneration proceeds. First there is the calling, to be followed by conviction. As I set this before you, you will not all too readily grasp it. I wish, however, that you would grasp it very clearly and that you would not need me to address you regarding this matter.

Regardless, however, the truth must remain the truth. If you are already converted, you must look into this mirror to reflect upon what God has done for you. We already have said that a person will come under conviction through a variety of means, such as a dream, an unexpected event, the sudden death of an acquaintance, or whatever else could be mentioned in this regard.

---

3. à Brakel is here using the word regeneration in its classic wider sense, which includes not only the transfer from death to life (i.e., regeneration in its narrow sense, as is commonly used today), but also the entire life of conversion that follows the initial regeneration.

4. Gen. 1:2.

However, the means unto conversion is the Word. "Of his own will he begot us by the word of truth" (James 1:18); "Being born again, not of corruptible seed, but of incorruptible, by the word of God, which lives and abides forever" (1 Peter 1:23).

When by means of the Word a person comes under conviction, he will think, "I cannot go on like this; I must be converted, or I cannot be saved." He will then begin to pray, "Oh, that I might be converted and saved!" This will even be accompanied by tears intended to move God to give him Jesus as well as faith in Him.

Children, do you see that such activity is still wrong and legalistic? This will readily become apparent. What happens to such persons who have been praying in such a fashion and therefore think of themselves as converted persons? Soon thereafter they will manifest themselves to the contrary. They will fall away, and though for a time they keep company with the godly, they will return to the world when the next opportunity affords itself. "It has happened unto them according to the true proverb, 'The dog is turned to his own vomit again and the sow that was washed to her wallowing in the mire.'"[5] At times such individuals become the greatest enemies of the life of godliness. Paul speaks of them in Hebrews 6:4–6: "For it is impossible for those who were once enlightened, and have tasted of the heavenly gift, and were made partakers of the Holy Ghost, and have tasted the good word of God, and the powers of the world to come, if they shall fall away, to renew them again unto repentance, since they crucify again for themselves the Son of God afresh, and put him to an open shame."

This applies to all who consider themselves to be converted. To presume ourselves to be converted without good reason is a devious device of Satan and our evil heart.

However, for others such conviction is followed by the gracious operation of the Spirit. I am now referring to the internal call, for the external call comes to all. In such situations, the Lord deals differently with each soul. In praying, such a soul meets with resistance. He no longer knows how to pray, and his heart stagnates when he desires to approach unto God, because he now sees things

---

5. 2 Peter 2:22.

in an entirely different light. He beholds God's holiness, knowing that God can have no fellowship with a sinner. He considers God's justice, recognizing that God cannot allow sin to go unpunished, and therefore he dares not to proceed. In fact, he perceives that it is impossible to come unto God apart from the satisfaction of a surety, and although he previously had heard of a surety, he now begins to perceive how very much he needs Him.

However, the matter is not yet resolved. They proceed and pray that for Jesus' sake they might be saved. They carefully seek to avoid sin so that they will not provoke Jesus to anger.

Oh, my friends, these are all grounds of our own making with which we must dispense if our experience is ever to be in truth! But the Lord now proceeds with such people and permits them to fall into great sin. That is grievous indeed, but for them this is sometimes very necessary. They will then be beside themselves, for all their broken reeds and sandy foundations are of no avail. How could they have fallen in such a fashion when their intentions had been so very different? Now they no longer know how to incline Jesus to be favorable toward them! Everything has fallen apart! What are they to do now?

Additionally, there will be various temptations. There will then be a voice within: "You have not been born again; you will not be saved; others are not as ungodly as you are; if the godly were to know who you really are, they would not tolerate you in their company."

They can be assaulted to such a degree that they fear they will lose their minds. Even their bodies can be affected to such an extent that haltingly they must go to Bethel. The fact that it takes so long to escape this quagmire has to do with the fact that the right spiritual exercises are lacking. When such a person finds himself in such a despondent condition, he will cry out, "There is nothing I can do, and I remain in bondage to sin. If ever I am to be saved, God will have to intervene," and here he arrives at the point where he will receive Jesus by faith in order to enter into covenant with Him. He will say, "If only Jesus would be there to help me! I now realize that it is true what He has said, 'Without me you can do nothing.' If only I could avail myself of His blood for cleansing!

If only He would be favorably inclined toward me! If only He would lead me out of these dreadful experiences!"[6]

This will finally yield sound spiritual exercises. Such persons become acquainted with Jesus as an all-sufficient surety who offers Himself to them for their salvation. The fact that some do not get beyond this point has to do with the fact that they do not begin where they ought to begin. They fail to see that a heartfelt surrender to the Lord Jesus to be saved in His way is also an act of faith.

At this point there will come increasing clarity. When the Lord Jesus beholds a person in that condition, as loathsome, despairing of self, and one whom no man pities, He will address such a person as He addressed that sick man at the pool of Bethesda, saying, "Will you be made whole?" Do you believe that I can do so? "Live! Yes, I said unto you when you were [struggling] in your own blood, Live."[7]

This is how Jesus becomes precious to this person and how his eyes are being opened. He receives clearer views of God's holiness, of the beauty of Jesus, and of his own wretched condition. He now views his misery with a clearer understanding. He beholds the justice of God and understands the impossibility of ever being reconciled with God apart from this surety.

He now becomes acquainted with Jesus in His person, in His offices, and in His states. He increasingly thinks about how exceedingly glorious it is to be reconciled with God, to have his sins forgiven, and to be in a state of grace. He exclaims, "Oh, what glorious matters these are!" There is progression after this—if you don't know this, learn it, and if you do know it, make good use of it—for Jesus reveals Himself to such ones in all His perfections, and He asks them whether they desire to have Him as such.

The issue will now be whether we say "yes." Jesus says, "Do you desire to be delivered from all the guilt, pollution, and punishment of sin?" Oh, friends, keep your heart engaged and consider yourself as being in the presence of God. Do you desire to be delivered from the wrath of God, the curse of the law, an accusing conscience, the

---

6. The biblical quotation in this paragraph is from John 15:5.
7. John 5:6 and Ezek. 16:6.

abuse of Satan, and eternal damnation? Is it indeed your desire to go your way in freedom, being delivered from the dominion of sin? Would that fully satisfy you?

Such a soul will reverently respond, "These are not the only things I desire, but rather, God must be my God and I must be His child. I must have intimate communion with Him, and I must sense that I cannot be without Him. And when He is absent from me, it must be to my credit to mourn about this absence, and grieving, to still follow the Lord and cleave unto Him (cf. Hos. 11:10; Ps. 63:9; 1 Sam. 7:2) until He again reveals Himself in His favor."

The Lord Jesus then says, "Do you wish to be delivered by my mighty arm not only from the dominion but also from the vestiges of sin? Do you not now deem it to be a blessing to wrestle prayerfully against the body of sin and death, and to do so in dependence upon my strength?"

Oh, that out of love to God and in obedience to His commandments you would continue on the way to heaven, to be in the presence of God forever as a weaned child and without your heart cleaving to this earth! Furthermore, do not expect your spiritual strength merely from the means of grace and not even from the most spiritual of ministers. Rather, while earnestly making use of the best of means, let your expectation be based only on the Lord's influence as you abide in the power of His grace and utter this heartfelt petition: "Teach me your way, O LORD; I will walk in your truth; unite my heart to fear your name." Do not these words arise in your heart: "O Lord, You and me, king and slave"?

The Lord Jesus also asks, "Is your complete salvation and desire dependent on the covenant of grace? Is fellowship with God all that you desire? Is evangelical holiness your heaven? Would you indeed be willing to deny everything in order to live for God alone? Would God's face have to shine upon you in all things to give you inner peace?"

If so, then hear this: The Lord Jesus, as a sweet-smelling savor to God, has given Himself as a sacrifice for sin for all His elect. He gives His blood unto atonement, His power for the deliverance from all enemies, and His Spirit as a pledge in order to seal, to comfort, and to lead them into all truth. And to all who live under the gospel and have been made desirous of these blessings, He says, "All of these I desire to give you. If you are desirous of these blessings, then I offer them to you in all sincerity and uprightness. Do indeed believe this! Come, you who are hungry and thirsty, stretch forth your hand, for now is the time to say 'yes.'"

Do not object by saying, "Anybody can say 'yes,'" for to this I reply that this is not so. It is not everyone who grieves over feeling and seeing his wretched condition, and it is not everyone who has an upright desire to live by faith in union with Christ and to the honor of the triune God! I am not speaking here of a sudden rush of emotion—even though it is a blessing if in some measure we have a natural inclination toward this—but this is what it is all about: the upright inclination of the heart and the voluntary and all-encompassing surrender of ourselves with soul and body to God and Christ, doing so upon His terms. Do not respond by saying that you would act too boldly in doing so, or that you do not know whether Jesus is calling you. In the preceding, I have already said enough about that, and I have attempted to make things clear. Instead, you should be troubled by your unbelief whereby you are making out the God of truth to be a liar by not embracing these proven and transparent evangelical truths.

But perhaps you have already given your heart to Jesus in this fashion long ago. If so, then do it consciously once more. I am hereby not saying that you should view yourself as not having had grace prior to doing this. Children of God, that would certainly not be true concerning you. Therefore, do not tamper with your foundation, but declare afresh, "Lord Jesus, do you desire to have me? My desire is toward you alone, and I thereby renounce all creatures."

Behold, this is the manner in which the Spirit draws when the call is extended. The effect of this is as powerful as we have described it, and regeneration then follows upon it.

I must speak of these matters in this sequence, for this is the way our mind relates to them. Regeneration naturally occurs first chronologically, it being a work of God in us. Faith then follows the work God has done in us. However, it is not so important whether the one is mentioned before the other, as long as your hearts are moved to surrender yourselves to Jesus.

Regeneration is therefore a complete transformation from death to life. It is because of sin that we are separated from God and are spiritually dead. The Lord, however, by the uncovering and drawing work of His Spirit not only gives us a lively understanding of the truth, but He also plants the principle of spiritual life in the soul. Take note that spiritual life neither primarily nor solely consists in deeds alone, but in this principle.

How then are we to define life? Philosophers give a good description of it when they say: "When I speak, listen, and look, for that is when an internal and living principle is at work; but it is not life itself." This is also applicable here. By virtue of union with God and Christ, the principle of spiritual life becomes operative. How shall I make this clear?

It is something that turns away from sin and all things related to it. It has an aversion for sin, and it is grieved when the old nature nevertheless is inclined toward sin and relishes it. It will oppose and resist that old nature as naturally as the sparks of fiery coals rise upward. It is a principle that turns Godward to obtain inner light, life, and joy. By faith such persons will approach God in Jesus, ceasing from their own works. Such persons will acquiesce in everything that Jesus asks of them, seeking through Him to become partakers of all these benefits and having confidence that He will do everything because He has called them.

With heart and soul such a person looks to the Lord alone, and will come as he is—polluted, sinful, and vile—saying, "Lord, are you willing to receive me as such? I cannot make any promises that I will not depart from you, and yet it is the commitment of my heart to abide with You. Lord, my eyes are focused upon these promises of Yours: 'I will put my fear in their hearts, that they shall not depart from me'[8]; 'I will take away the stony heart out of your flesh, and I will give you a heart of flesh.'[9] Amen, Lord, and may your words be fulfilled, for you who have begun a good work will also finish it."

---

8. Jer. 32:40.
9. Ezek. 36:26.

This is the manner in which a person becomes one of the blessed ones who trusts in the Lord. In Hebrew, faith is occasionally designated by a word that is the equivalent of allowing oneself to be carried like a suckling infant that quietly entrusts itself to its wet-nurse.

In like fashion, a soul entrusts herself to the arms of the all-sufficient Jehovah, allowing itself to be led and carried with confidence as it pleases Him. If the way for her is free of obstacles, then the holier the better. If, however, the way is muddy and rough, as it was for Israel while traveling through the wilderness to Canaan, then this is agreeable as well. With unconditional surrender she only prays, "Lord, teach and guide me, and cause me to walk before your face."

If this disposition truly is yours, we may assure you that you are in a state of grace. Gratefully acknowledge this in your inner chamber, and do not despise the day of small things, for the Almighty One has done nothing less than work a gracious miracle on you and within you.

You may consider it to be problematic if you cannot say at what precise moment you were drawn to God. There will be thousands in heaven who were not able to relate the exact moment of their conversion. Many of them failed to consider their spiritual exercises calmly and considered a work of conviction and preparation to be the true work of regeneration.

You also need not be concerned if your conviction has not been as deep and lengthy as with others. It is sufficient if you have been stripped of all false foundations and as a naked sinner have come to Jesus, for the Lord is sovereign as to how He deals with each.

There are some who have very deep convictions, such as the jailor and as Paul, who neither ate nor drank for three days. Others, such as Zacchaeus, have but gentle convictions. Also, be not concerned as to how you will fare in the future. All will be well with you, for there is life!

And how does such life become evident? By way of light. Previously there was also light that resulted in conviction. However, this was followed by increasing light and discernment, though not all at once. It resembles the rising of the sun. Initially it is pitch black, and then light begins to glimmer. There is little or no light, but then the light begins to shine with increasing clarity, and it continues until the day has fully dawned.

How does such a soul conduct herself when light begins to arise? The world then becomes despicable to her, and what once appeared so delightful to her has now become loathsome. That which she previously loved she now hates, and she now loves what she previously hated. Her desires and inclinations are now entirely different, and she says, "O, if only I could have God as my portion!" She now wishes to pray in total dependency upon the will of the Lord and to His honor. It is now her delight in all things to lean upon her beloved. With Him, she would even be willing to walk through the night, and when indwelling corruption manifests itself and when she is inwardly tempted to withdraw from Him, she is nevertheless assured that the Lord will keep His Word: "I will never leave you or forsake you."[10] She has denied everything for Jesus' sake. He called her, she came, and she said "Yes" to him. He has seen all her struggles, her sorrow, and her troubles until all of this taught her to surrender everything into His hands.

Is it presently so that it appears to you as if your pathway is not directed toward Canaan and as if He has forgotten you? Then let this indeed be a matter of concern for you, but do not discredit your spiritual state on account of it. Permit the Lord to direct your steps, and if it pleases Him to manifest His love toward you, it is well. However, if it pleases Him to lead you in a way of darkness, then it is also well. Let nothing but His good pleasure be your sole delight. Persevere in seeking the Lord. And friends, let me add that he who can pray ought never to complain.

This will be followed by conduct that is markedly different. Such a person will no longer be satisfied that he refrains from evil and practices that which is good, but rather, all that has not been done as in the presence of God will no longer be delightful to him. It becomes his desire to act in pure filial obedience, and if this is not his motive, he finds no delight in it.

---

10. Heb. 13:5.

This also results in choosing social fellowship that is of an entirely different nature. Are you still at ease in worldly company? Are your bosom friends to be found in that environment? Do you consider it to be an act of civility to be everyone's friend? If so, then believe me that you are still unconverted. Granted, a Christian will manifest a measure of civility, and his moderation should be known to all men. However, it ought not to have a worldly flavor.

Do not object that in order to live such a life you have to remove yourself from the world or that your nature is still what it is and that it is permissible to have a winsome and pleasant character. To this I respond that if your profession is intertwined with such worldly company so that it is impossible but that you must commit sin, then you have an occupation that is not suitable for you. However, if such interaction is but incidental, then it remains true that there must always be a distance between you and the world, for "the righteous is more excellent than his neighbor."[11] If necessity dictates that you must be in company with worldly people, as may often be the case, then this must nevertheless be in your heart: "Woe is me, that I sojourn in Mesech"; "Depart from me, ye evildoers"; "I am a companion of all them that fear the Lord."[12]

Love for God's people yields a clear mark that a person is in a state of grace, for we know that whosoever loves God will also love his brother.[13]

You may say that if this is a clear mark of grace, then there are indeed many godly people, for many unconverted people do not hate the godly. Some even try to employ godly servants. To this I respond that they do this not because they love the godly for their godliness, but because they have a sweet character or a tender conscience, and will not defraud anyone. However, if we love the godly because of their virtues, although they may subscribe to an opinion differing from ours, if we love them even when they are hated by everyone—including by the wise and wealthy of this

---

11. Prov. 12:26.
12. Ps. 120:5; Ps. 119:115; and Ps. 119:63.
13. 1 John 4:21.

world—and if loving them brings us harm rather than advantage, then this is a clear mark of godliness.

Therefore, people of God, in conclusion, does not this describe your conduct? From eternal election proceeds the calling, and from this issues forth both regeneration and faith with its fruits, including love for the brothers. What rich opportunity I have here to pronounce this people blessed! They are the precious children of Zion, to be esteemed of greater value than fine gold. They are a people who are born of God, partakers of the heavenly calling, yes, partakers of the divine nature who have God as their Father.[14] What a great matter it is indeed to have received the adoption of sons![15] With such faith we must against hope believe in hope.[16] Live, therefore, to the glory of God the Father. Magnify the free grace manifested to you in Christ. Freely exclaim: Abba, Father, my Father, who has known me in Your eternal love and has delivered me from the power of darkness, and has translated me into the kingdom of His dear Son.[17]

Believe, therefore, also that God, being your Father in Christ, will care for you as His beloved children. And thus say: "God my Father shall have pity upon me in all my struggles. He shall hear my prayers in accordance with His will, and I will unburden my heart to Him as my Father. Joyfully I will ask for all that I am lacking, trusting that He who has begun a good work in me will not forsake me. He shall guide me with His counsel, and afterward receive me to glory. There I shall see my beloved Jesus and speak to Him, doing so mouth to mouth. There I will sing an everlasting hallelujah." Oh, it will be a salvation that is inexpressible and beyond our comprehension! Children of the Lord, all of this will be your portion. "And every man that has this hope in him purifies himself, even as he is pure."[18]

May the Almighty bless what has been spoken to His glory. Amen.

---

14. Heb. 3:1 and 2 Peter 1:4.
15. Gal. 4:5.
16. Rom. 4:18.
17. Col. 1:14.
18. 1 John 3:3.

Dutch Reformed
Translation Society

"The Heritage of the Ages for Today"
P.O. Box 7083
Grand Rapids, MI 49510

Board of Directors

Dr. Joel Beeke
president and professor of systematic theology and homiletics
Puritan Reformed Theological Seminary
Grand Rapids, MI

Dr. Gerald M. Bilkes
professor of Old and New Testament
Puritan Reformed Theological Seminary
Grand Rapids, MI

Dr. John Bolt
professor of systematic theology
Calvin Theological Seminary
Grand Rapids, MI

Professor Ronald Cammenga
professor of dogmatics and Old Testament studies
Protestant Reformed Theological Seminary
Grand Rapids, MI

Jay T. Collier
director of publishing
Reformation Heritage Books
Grand Rapids, MI

Dr. James A. De Jong
president and professor of historical theology, emeritus
Calvin Theological Seminary
Grand Rapids, MI

Dr. I. John Hesselink
Albertus C. Van Raalte Professor of Systematic Theology, emeritus
Western Theological Seminary
Holland, MI

Paul Heule
CEO, Eenhoorn LLC
Grand Rapids, MI

Dr. Earl Wm. Kennedy
senior research fellow
A. C. Van Raalte Institute
Holland, MI

James R. Kinney
director of Baker Academic
Baker Book House Company
Grand Rapids, MI

Dr. Nelson Kloosterman
professor of ethics and New Testament studies
Mid-America Reformed Seminary
Dyer, IN

The board gratefully acknowledges the financial support of individual patrons, foundations, and academic institutions that met the costs of this translation.

Lifetime membership in the Dutch Reformed Translation Society is available for a one-time, tax-deductible gift of $100. Members support the society's continuing work, receive periodic newsletters, and may purchase society publications at the cost of production. Membership gifts may be sent to P.O. Box 7083, Grand Rapids, MI 49510.